WINNING YOUR PERSONAL INJURY CLAIM

WINNING YOUR PERSONAL INJURY CLAIM

with sample forms

and worksheets

———

Evan K. Aidman

Attorney at Law

Sourcebooks
Inc.
Naperville, IL • Clearwater, FL

Published by: **Sourcebooks, Inc.**

Naperville Office
P.O. Box 372
Naperville, Illinois 60566
(630) 961-3900
FAX: 630-961-2168

Clearwater Office
P.O. Box 25
Clearwater, Florida 33757
(813) 587-0999
FAX: 813-586-5088

Cover Design: Andrew Sardina/Dominique Raccah
Interior Design and Production: Andrew Sardina, Sourcebooks, Inc.

This publication is designed to provide accurate and authoritative information in regard to the subject matter covered. It is sold with the understanding that the publisher is not engaged in rendering legal, accounting, or other professional service. If legal advice or other expert assistance is required, the services of a competent professional person should be sought.
From a Declaration of Principles Jointly Adopted by a Committee of the
American Bar Association and a Committee of Publishers and Associations

Library of Congress Cataloging-in-Publication Data
Aidman, Evan K., 1958-
    Winning your personal injury claim: with sample forms and worksheets/Evan K. Aidman.
        p.   cm.
    Includes index.
    ISBN 1-57071-165-8 (pbk.)
    1. Personal injuries—United States—Popular works.   I. Title.
KF1257.Z9A38   1997
346.7303'23—dc21   97-16712
                                                                                                                CIP

Printed and bound in the United States of America.
Paperback — 10 9 8 7 6 5 4 3 2 1

To Mom, Jeanne Whitehouse Aidman

CONTENTS

USING SELF-HELP LAW BOOKS

Whenever you shop for a product or service, you face various levels of quality and price. In deciding what product or service to buy, you make a cost/value analysis on the basis of your willingness to pay and the quality you desire.

When buying a car, you decide whether you want transportation, comfort, status, or sex appeal. Accordingly, you decide among such choices as a Neon, a Lincoln, a Rolls Royce, or a Porsche. Before making a decision, you usually weigh the merits of each option against the cost.

When you have a headache, you can take a pain reliever (such as aspirin) or visit a medical specialist for a neurological examination. Given this choice, most people, of course, take a pain reliever, since it costs only pennies, whereas a medical examination costs hundreds of dollars and takes a lot of time. This is usually a logical choice, because rarely is anything more than a pain reliever needed for a headache. But, in some cases, a headache may indicate a brain tumor, and failing to see a specialist right away can result in complications. Should everyone with a headache go to a specialist? Of course not, but people who treat their own illnesses must realize that they are betting on the basis of their cost/value analysis of the situation, they are taking the most logical option.

The same cost/value analysis must be made in deciding to do one's own legal work. Many legal situations are very straightforward, requiring a simple form and no complicated analysis. Anyone with a little intelligence and a book of instructions can handle the matter without outside help.

But there is always the chance that complications are involved that only an attorney would notice. To simplify the law into a book like this, several legal cases often must be condensed into a single sentence or paragraph. Otherwise, the book would be several hundred pages long and too complicated for most people. However, this simplification necessarily leaves out many details and nuances that would apply to special or unusual situations. Also, there are many ways to interpret most legal questions. Your case may come before a judge who disagrees with this analysis.

Therefore, in deciding to use a self-help law book and to do your own legal work, you must realize that you are making a cost/value analysis. You need to weigh the chance that your case will not turn out to your satisfaction against the money you will save by doing it yourself. Most people who handle their own simple legal matters never have a problem, but people occasionally find that they ended up paying more to have an attorney straighten out the situation than it would have if they had hired an attorney in the beginning. Keep this in mind while handling your case, and be sure to consult an attorney if you feel you might need further guidance.

INTRODUCTION

The most common complaint against personal injury attorneys is that they don't communicate with their clients. Again and again individuals complain that their lawyer won't return their telephone calls. It is easy to imagine the anxiety the layperson must feel when questions about his or her lawsuit go unanswered. The personal injury litigation process is an extremely complicated and emotionally charged affair. The client's need for accurate information about it and clarification on the myriad of issues surrounding it is legitimate and real. I hope this book will answer many of those questions and will put to rest many of the anxieties associated with this process. If your lawyer fails to answer your questions or clarify your case, this book may help you get his or her attention.

The litigation savvy you will acquire from this book will enable you to ask your lawyer sophisticated questions about your case. This may well trigger his or her interest in you and your case. Of course, it is inexcusable for your lawyer to ignore your calls or to "backburner" your case. Nevertheless, today's overworked, burnt-out P.I. (Personal Injury) lawyer may do just that unless you can set yourself apart from his or her other clients with the knowledge you gain from this book. If all else fails, you should consider firing your attorney and finding one who will work with you. See Chapter 3 for an in-depth discussion of that topic.

If you would like to communicate with me about this book, you may reach me toll free by calling (888) 860-1600. The six digit code to dial after the prompt is 956902. You can also reach me by telephone at my Pennsylvania office by dialing (610) 359-1919 or at my New Jersey office by dialing (609) 338-1166. You can fax me at (610) 359-0761 or you can contact me by E-mail at EVKENT@ AOL.COM. I look forward to hearing from you.

PERSONAL INJURY LITIGATION

Everyone these days has an opinion about personal injury litigation. Many people feel that the right to sue for injuries should be severely limited in hopes that this will bring down insurance costs. Others feel that this right should not be so limited. They fear that legislation enacted to restrict the right to sue will make big business, the insurance industry, and medical practitioners less accountable to the public. They also fear the loss of financial compensation for injuries caused by a negligent or careless act. The only constant seems to be an interest in the debate and an interest in trials.

The O.J. Simpson trials prove beyond a reasonable doubt that Americans crave insight into trials, trial lawyers, and legal conflict. Personal injury litigation, while not as inherently glamorous as litigation involving someone like O.J. Simpson, has its own drama and fascination. In my years as a personal injury trial lawyer, I have accumulated a considerable amount of experience and awareness of courtroom drama. In this book I share with you my special insights into "P.I. litigation." I hope it serves as a legal compass which you can use to steer yourself toward the remedies available to enforce your rights.

To begin with, the term "litigation" creates some degree of confusion. Litigation involves far more than just the trial of a legal conflict. It also extends beyond pre-trial activities such as depositions and the discovery process. Personal injury litigation begins the moment the accident occurs. Every word that is exchanged and every thought that is processed thereafter plays a part in the ultimate event: the settlement or trial of a personal injury case. The skillful trial lawyer begins litigating, that is, crafting ideas that will work toward a successful resolution of the case, from the very first contact with the client. Anything less is lazy lawyering; perhaps even malpractice.

In this book I examine every aspect of personal injury litigation, from car insurance choices to jury trials and beyond. The laws applicable to personal injury vary from state to state, notwithstanding the efforts of Congress to place nationwide limits on the amounts that can be collected through litigation. Much of the information I present involves general principles of law. The law or practice in your state may be different. Nevertheless, there is much uniformity throughout the states regarding personal injury litigation. Most of the information in this book can be used by personal injury litigants in any state. Where I cite matters that apply to litigants in a particular state, I make this clear. You may have to refer to local sources for the law or practice that applies to your particular situation.

One of the beauties of the law is that it is dynamic and ever-changing. The law is flexible enough to accommodate a changing world. When the first automobile accident occurred, the judge didn't have a problem because there were no automobile laws; he used the legal logic of horse and buggy cases. Similarly, when new technologies cause injuries in the future, the law will be flexible enough to accommodate them.

The federal and state legislatures are constantly passing new laws that apply to personal injury litigation. The courts rule every day on disputes that require interpretation of new laws as well as laws that have been on the books for many years. When a court decides a dispute, the court's ruling becomes "precedent" for the future. In other words, the interpretations they dispense become the law by which future litigants can be guided. Because the law is ever-changing and growing, you should keep in mind that you may have legal rights that you are unaware of which an attorney could point out to you. Therefore, in all but the simplest cases you would be well-advised to consult with a lawyer concerning the law applicable to your case. I do not recommend that you rely on this book alone. My words to you here are a guide and a starting point only.

What to do After an Accident 1

At the Scene of an Accident

The actions you take at the scene of any accident are of utmost importance in determining the course of your personal injury litigation. Whether you have been injured in a car collision, a slip and fall accident, as the result of equipment failure, by a doctor's negligence or in any other way, you must, during the very earliest stages, take great care in everything you say and do. Never again will your memory of the key events be as fresh as they are on the day of injury. Never again will the most crucial bits of evidence be as available. Thus, you must concentrate totally on what has happened to you, all aspects of the accident scene, and you must act quickly to insure that the information you gather at the scene of the injury is preserved for your use throughout the litigation.

The events that occur right after a car accident can determine whether the injured victim receives fair and prompt compensation. Extreme care must be taken to avoid saying anything which could later be interpreted as an admission of fault. An insurance company lawyer can even turn an apology uttered during this stressful time into an admission. By the same token, listen carefully to what the occupants of the other vehicle say, and write down key admissions as soon as possible. Often, people make statements at accident scenes during the heat of the moment which, given time for reflection, they would not make. The key is to avoid discussing the cause of the accident.

It is always a good idea to call the police to the scene. Failure to do so can lead an insurance company to deny that an accident ever happened! Photographs of your car, before it is repaired, help to defeat this argument. Do not leave the scene until you are sure you or the police have all of the other driver's identifying information. This includes the vehicle tag (license plate) number, name, address, driver's license number, the name of his or her insurance company and the policy number. Ask if the driver is "on the clock" for his or her employer. If so, the employer may be liable for the damages. Ask the police officer for a copy of the police report. Be aware of any circumstance or condition relating in any way to the cause of the accident. For example, check for skid marks, accident debris, etc. If you hire an attorney, be sure to let him or her know what you have found.

It is also vital that you get the name, address, and phone number of any eyewitnesses to the accident. People are often reluctant to get involved. However, most people will respond if you appeal to their sense of justice and fair play. Without the assistance of a witness, it may be impossible for you to obtain fair compensation for your injuries. Most people can put themselves in the shoes of an accident victim who needs the help of a witness.

You may think that fault for the accident is absolutely clear. Unfortunately, insurance companies deny claims for practically any reason at all. If the other motorist does not admit fault, your claim can be tied up for years in litigation. A solid eyewitness statement, especially by someone you've never met before, is easily the most effective way to convince an insurance company to honor your claim. Insurance companies are particularly persuaded by statements made by truly independent witnesses.

Witnesses are perhaps even more important in "fall down" accident cases. Insurance companies are often suspicious of this kind of accident since property damage, which substantiates auto accidents, is not present. Thus, a prompt investigation, which includes witness statements and photographs of the accident scene, will go a long way towards convincing the insurance company that it should pay fair and prompt compensation.

Form 1 in the Appendix of this book is a worksheet for recording important car accident information. You should complete this form as soon after the accident as possible. Form 2 is a fall down accident worksheet.

EMERGENCY ROOM TREATMENT

If you have been injured in an accident, the first place you should go is to a hospital emergency room. Regardless of how you feel, go to the E. R. to get yourself checked out. You may be in shock and not even realize the severity of the trauma. Many people feel no pain until the next morning when they often report feeling like they've just been beaten up. Going to the E. R. is not only a good idea from a health standpoint, it also helps to convince the insurance company that you were injured.

Insurance companies place special credence on the E. R. report, since the hospital's description of the accident and injuries is generally made before much, if any, consideration has been given to litigation and lawyers. You, therefore, need to be extra careful that everything you say to the medical providers is accurate. E. R. doctors and nurses often are extremely busy and may have little interest in accurately documenting the details of the accident. Unfortunately, the mistakes they make can come back to haunt you. The insurance company may feel that the version noted in the E. R. is accurate, even if it is not. While your family doctor may be willing to correct a mistake in a report, the E. R. doctor probably will not. So, again, be clear and accurate when describing your injuries to the emergency room staff.

Form 10 in the Appendix of this book is a worksheet for keeping track of all the treatment you receive after an accident. You should use this to keep an accurate record throughout your recovery.

BEWARE THE FRIENDLY INSURANCE ADJUSTER

During the period immediately after an accident, the insurance companies involved with the case will likely try to engage you in discussions concerning your accident. You simply cannot be too careful when dealing with an insurance company, especially if you are not represented by a lawyer. This is true whether you are contacted by your company or by the company of the person who injured you. Perhaps a certain horror story will illustrate this point.

I had a client come to me several years ago who had already signed a release with the insurance company and accepted a small sum of money in exchange. (See Form 22 for a sample Release.) This took place a few short weeks after the accident. I was still able to negotiate an additional, substantial settlement with the insurance company, even though releases typically discharge the company from any further liability.

I was able to accomplish this feat by proving that my client lacked the mental capacity to understand the nature of the document he signed. I was able to prove that he went to see his psychologist in an extremely distraught state of mind on the very day the he signed release. His thoughts were racing and jumbled, his heartbeat was elevated, he was sweating and trembling, etc. He had experienced multiple blows to his head in the accident and sustained a concussion. Just before the trial was to begin the insurance company agreed to provide adequate compensation for the injuries suffered. I think the company feared the anger a jury would feel at this company for taking advantage of an unrepresented and emotionally vulnerable person.

This was a fortunate result, since it is very difficult to void a signed release. The lesson here is to watch out for "friendly" insurance adjusters bearing legal documents.

Especially if you are injured by an uninsured or underinsured motorist, your interests and those of your insurance company will conflict. In this situation, you will seek compensation for your pain and suffering from your own insurance company. (See Chapter 10 for a discussion of uninsured and underinsured motorist benefits.) Also, in every auto accident case, it is your own insurer who pays your medical bills and lost wages. This insurer's investigation of the accident is centered around avoiding any financial payout. It is vital that you contact a legal advocate whose only interest is to obtain maximum compensation for you.

Your insurance company may also send you "tips" about what you should do after an accident. I recently received such a mailing from my own insurance company. A review of this information will be helpful to you.

My insurance company advises that there are some easy steps that should be followed at the scene of an accident. Many of these helpful hints are quite good. They include calling the police, not admitting fault at the scene of the accident, exchanging insurance information with the other driver, obtaining the other driver's name, address, phone number, license plate number, etc. The final suggestion is to notify your insurance agent promptly. Indeed, your policy obligates you to place your insurance company on notice of an accident. However, this should be done by your attorney if anyone was seriously injured.

If you submit to a tape-recorded statement for your insurer or fill out claims forms without the aid of counsel, you may well make mistakes which will compromise your claim. Do not underestimate the devious nature of some employees of some insurance companies. They are well trained to investigate accident cases so as to defend against fraudulent and exaggerated claims. That is obviously appropriate and to the greater good of the insurance company and society as a whole. However, the unsuspecting and uncounseled individual frequently will fall prey to the trickster insurance agent who seeks to protect the insurance company's pocketbook at the expense of the legitimate claimant.

I have seen insurance companies misrepresent the amount of their policy limits in order to settle cases for far less than justified by the nature of the injuries. I have heard of insurance adjusters advising claimants to avoid getting an attorney because the lawyer would supposedly take all of the money. And I have seen insurance representatives place settlement agreements before unrepresented claimants, advising them that the papers applied to property damage only. In reality, the document was a general release discharging all liability for any type of insurance claim arising out of the accident. I am currently handling such a case. I expect that I will be able to void the agreement, but not without an ugly, time-consuming, and completely unnecessary battle.

While there are many hardworking and honest insurance representatives, bad apples exist. You lose nothing by calling your lawyer first for a free consultation after an accident. It is just the wise and safe road to travel.

DON'T SIGN ANYTHING!

Besides the insurance adjuster, you may get phone calls from attorneys, private investigators, and others offering to "help" you and asking you to sign a contract for their services. Don't sign anything until you have time to recover from the injury, think clearly, and perhaps discuss the situation with someone who can give you an unbiased opinion.

Some states have laws forbidding lawyers from contacting victims for 30 days after an accident, but that doesn't always stop them. With the possibility of millions of dollars in legal fees, lawyers have been known to fly to accident scenes to solicit business from hospital waiting rooms and airports. Those not as bold send their employees and agents to "give solace" to victims and pass out their cards. One man even dressed like a priest while consoling the victims and suggesting they consult his employing attorney.

Almost all personal injury attorneys will give you an initial consultation at no charge to evaluate your case. Such an appointment gives the attorney a chance to decide if your case is worth his or her time. But it can also be your chance to find out if you have a case and if the attorney is someone you feel comfortable with.

There is no harm in making an appointment with such an attorney as soon as you feel well enough to do so. However, you should not feel pressured to sign any agreement with the first attorney you visit. Tell him or her that you don't feel ready to sign anything immediately, but that you will call when you are ready.

If you do not feel comfortable with the first attorney you meet with, you should see one or two others. As long as they agree to consult with you without charge, you have nothing to lose but a little of your time.

REMEMBER THE DEADLINE!

While people are eager to take care of their injury right after the accident, as time goes on and weeks turn into months it is easy to forget how much time has passed. If the other side takes weeks to answer your letter, and it takes you weeks to gather all the medical information requested, a year can pass before you realize it.

It is important to keep track of time, because each state has a law regarding how long you can wait before filing suit. It is in the best interest of the other side or their insurance company to delay the case until the deadline has passed. Don't let this happen to you, or you will lose your claim.

The shortest limit of any state is one year. In other states it is as long as 6 years. This is from the time of the accident until the day a lawsuit is filed. Sometimes if the deadline is approaching and settlement is near an insurance adjuster will try to delay past the limitation. In such a case a lawsuit must be filed to keep the case alive.

There is further discussion of statutes of limitations in Chapter 7.

Should You Hire a Lawyer? 2

Can You Handle Your Case without a Lawyer?

There are some types of cases that should not be settled without using the services of an attorney, and others that you may be able to handle yourself. The advantage of using an attorney is that he or she is experienced at obtaining a full settlement from an insurance company or defendant, and should know how much your claim is worth. The disadvantage is that the attorney's fee can be as much as half of your award after costs and other fees are added.

Simple cases, where the injury is minor and the fault clear, can often be settled quickly with the insurance company without hiring an attorney. Even if the company balks at paying, you can often get a good settlement by filing a small claims case, since the insurance company's expense of going to court is often higher than the cost of settling. Complicated cases, such as with serious medical malpractice or an accident causing death, should be handled by an attorney who can analyze the value of the case and let the other side know that you are serious about your claim.

As a personal injury attorney I have seen people who have made the mistake of settling their case without adequate legal advice. It is my firm belief that almost all personal injury litigants should seek counsel. But the purpose of this book is to give you the information you need to handle your case, with or without a lawyer. Therefore I will do my best to explain what you can expect if you act on your own.

Perhaps another true story will help illustrate the stresses of litigating without counsel. I was recently contacted by a client who is an employee of an insurance company. This person's familiarity with insurance practice tempted her to forego using an attorney to handle her injury case. I advised her that I would be happy to consult with her without charge but that I preferred that she actually retain my services. She was reluctant since she felt that she could perhaps do better financially by herself. She was worried that my percentage of the settlement would leave her with less money than if she handled the case herself.

About two months later this client contacted me again in a highly emotional state of mind. The combined stress of being injured and dealing one-on-one with the insurance company had left her psychologically scarred and physically drained. Her physical and emotional condition improved immediately upon retaining my services. By relinquishing control of her case she was also able to let go of pressures that were hindering her healing process. This client did not express a single regret during the entire course of her case about her decision to retain my services. Even when I deducted my share from the settlement proceeds, she expressed nothing but gratitude.

THE BEST OF BOTH WORLDS

I was also recently contacted by an individual who had managed to obtain an offer of $50,000 to settle his son's case. This person wanted to know if it was safe to take the money without retaining a lawyer. He was afraid that, if a lawyer were brought into the case, the lawyer might settle the case for $55,000 and take one third of the proceeds. My advice was to meet with several lawyers in order to work out the best possible arrangement. I told the client to insist that the first $50,000 was for his son and that the lawyer's fee would come out of any amount he could negotiate above and beyond that amount.

This is a creative solution to a seemingly difficult problem. You need to think your situation through carefully so that you can come up with these kinds of solutions. There are plenty of unscrupulous lawyers who will steal you blind if you don't act with care. These kinds of creative solutions will win you the respect of the lawyer you finally retain.

It is an illusion to think that an insurance company will offer an unrepresented person the same kind of settlement money it would offer a person represented by a capable personal injury lawyer. There is virtually no way for you to know the value of a personal injury case. These values are based upon years of jury verdicts and insurance settlements. Only an experienced personal injury attorney can accurately assess the maximum amount an insurance company is likely to pay for a particular injury.

The company knows very well that it possesses superior knowledge and bargaining power. It will not hesitate to use this knowledge and power to its advantage and your disadvantage. Insurance companies pay only what they feel they will be compelled to pay by a jury. A strong personal injury lawyer on your side acts like a hammer over the head of the insurance company. The company pays far more when it fears the outcome that an experienced personal injury attorney can secure for the client. Insurance companies do not fear unrepresented individuals because such individuals lack knowledge about how to inflict pain upon the company if it does not settle the case. It's like fighting a war without modern weapons. The other side is not likely to listen seriously to your terms of surrender if you have no ability to effectively wage the battle.

The insurance company will also know that, even if the facts and justice are on your side, your unfamiliarity with the legal procedures involved may allow the company to beat your claim on a legal technicality.

Although the courts generally relax the rules of procedure for unrepresented parties, you can't count on this. The rules are made by lawyers for use by lawyers. It is extremely hard to dot all the i's and cross all the t's in just the right way when it comes to a personal injury lawsuit. Again, my advice is to retain an honest, energetic personal injury specialist at the first possible opportunity.

Cases involving property damage alone can be settled fairly without the assistance of an attorney. It may be better here to handle the case yourself and spare yourself the expense of an attorney. There are books available that set forth the value of cars. These accepted values establish guidelines that the insurance company should follow. There are no such clear-cut guidelines concerning the "value" of pain and suffering in a serious injury case. That's why you need a lawyer.

HANDLING YOUR CASE WITHOUT A LAWYER

Okay, so you've decided your case is simple and clear-cut enough to settle without hiring an attorney. Now what? Keep in mind that you are the only non-lawyer who is permitted to handle your case. Even though your cousin Bernie thinks he can represent you as well as any real lawyer, the law does not allow that. It's called "the unauthorized practice of law." Bernie can give you all the "off the record" helpful hints he wants, but if you do not retain a licensed attorney, you must sign all of the official court documents yourself and you must appear in court yourself. If you are sure you want to attempt this, there are certain tips I can give you to help ease your way.

First off, please review Chapter 1 of this book. My advice about the events that occur immediately after an accident applies whether you intend to retain a lawyer or not. This is because these events take place before an attorney is contacted. Next, in auto accident cases always obtain the police report. You even have an advantage here over people who are represented by attorneys. The police, especially big city police, often will more readily and more rapidly turn over their information to you, the accident victim, than they will to a lawyer. The police report is crucial because it contains the names, addresses, and phone numbers of witnesses, insurance information for the person who injured you, license numbers, a diagram of the accident, and many other important items.

PHOTOGRAPHS
The police may even have photographs of the accident scene and the cars. Of course, you should get copies of any photographs. Or be sure to take your own if the damage to the cars was more than minimal. Photographs of the accident scene should always be taken if there is any doubt as to who caused the accident. If you were rear-ended, you probably don't need photos of the scene of the accident. If you were injured in a "slip and fall" accident, photos of the area where you fell are absolutely, positively essential. These should be taken as soon after the accident as possible. Once the ice you slipped on melts, your testimony may be the only proof that it existed.

RESCUE REPORT
If you were taken from the accident scene by an ambulance or other paratransit vehicle, you should obtain the rescue report. This report may contain useful information prepared by the rescue workers. The rescue report may document your distress at the accident scene. It may also provide data regarding the condition of the scene itself, although generally the police report is far more helpful in that respect.

WITNESSES
You should contact witnesses as soon as possible after the accident. Memories fade rapidly, so speed is important. Also, your adversary's insurance company will probably try to contact witnesses as well. It's always better for you to reach an important witness first. A crafty insurance investigator may be able to convince an otherwise favorable witness that perhaps his view of the accident wasn't so favorable to you. So don't wait. Speed is of the essence.

If the witness is favorable to you, be sure to prepare a written statement for him or her to sign. This statement should be an accurate recitation of his or her view of the events of the accident. Some people are reluctant to be witnesses. If you sense reluctance, let the witness know that you do not plan to retain a lawyer. This may increase the sympathy the witness has for you since he or she may feel that you really need his or her help. The witness may also appreciate being able to deal directly with you rather than having to work through a lawyer. A lot of people simply don't like dealing with lawyers, so again, your being unrepresented can be an advantage here.

FIRST CONTACT

Once you have completed your investigation of the accident, contact the insurer for the person or company you are making your claim against. You can use a letter similar to the one I use to make first contact with the insurance company. (See Form 6.) If you do not know who the insurer is, the first letter should go to the person or business you are suing. (See Form 7.) You can use certified mail, which tends to increase the attention the recipient pays to your letter. Certainly if you get no response to this first contact letter, the follow-up letter should be sent by certified mail. By all means have the letter prepared in a professional way and be sure there are no typos. You are trying to create an image of competence and seriousness. A handwritten or poorly typed letter with mistakes will reduce the value of your case in the eyes of the insurance company.

RECORDED STATEMENTS

When you are contacted by the insurance company, be on your guard. The claim representative or insurance investigator will salivate at the idea that you are unrepresented. He or she has got all the advantages of experience and litigation savvy. The investigator may try, right off the bat, to take a written or tape-recorded statement from you. Don't permit this under any circumstances. He or she is looking to pin you down in order to trap you into a position which later you may wish you weren't in. It's name, rank, and serial number only at this point. Don't get into too many details. There will be plenty of time for that if a lawsuit is required. If you feel that you simply must give a recorded statement to the insurance company, insist on the right to take a recorded statement from the person who injured you. That's only fair. If the insurance company refuses, then you know they don't intend to fight fair.

You should probably get a lawyer in any case where recorded statements are going to be taken. But if you are dead set on representing yourself and you're willing to give a recorded statement to the insurance company, then take care. This statement can come back to haunt you. You will be asked numerous and detailed questions about the accident and your medical care. Form 11 is an outline of the types of questions you can expect. Think through how you will answer these questions before you give the statement. Be sure to see the section on "Depositions" in Chapter 8. A deposition is a question and answer session that takes place after a lawsuit is filed. The suggestions in Chapter 8 apply equally to pre-lawsuit statements. If you have a tape recorder you should record your own testimony so that you can recollect what you said at a later date. If you later hire an attorney, he or she will want to know what you said.

MEDICAL TREATMENT

During the time that all of this investigative activity is going on, you should also be receiving medical treatment for your injuries. Without treatment, the insurance company assumes that you weren't hurt. More importantly, medical treatment, especially during the first months after the accident, is the best way to assure a rapid recovery from your injuries. Keep all of your medical appointments. Be sure your doctors have accurate information about the accident itself so that their reports do not contain errors. The insurance company's lawyer will use erroneous medical bills or reports against you during the trial. If there are errors, call the doctor to get a corrected bill or report.

KEEPING A JOURNAL

It is a good idea to keep a journal of your daily activities and how the accident has affected you. Be sure to note how your pain progresses. It is easy later for this painful period to slip out of your mind. When your trial finally arrives, the diary will be a godsend. It will refresh your memory of your pain and recuperation period like nothing else. If you are unable to communicate your pain to the jury, you can't expect to receive full compensation. That is why a journal is important, whether you have an attorney or not.

When your treatment begins to wind down, you should start gathering the medical documentation. Your medical bills and reports should be gathered, organized, reviewed for accuracy and sent to the insurance company with a settlement offer. Form 8 and Form 9 are examples of letters you can send to doctors and hospitals when you need medical records.

Determining what to settle your case for is one of the most difficult problems you will face. Chapter 6 discusses the settlement process and the methods professionals use to evaluate cases. I suggest that you review that chapter carefully. You most likely will not be able to negotiate a settlement as large as a lawyer might. The insurance company fears the jury verdict an experienced personal injury attorney is capable of getting far more than one an unrepresented plaintiff can get. In addition the company knows that it can take advantage of your inexperience throughout the litigation process. Your lack of familiarity with court procedures can be fatal to your case. Thus, you should not expect to negotiate as successfully as a lawyer.

It is still possible for you to do better financially *without* a lawyer. If you have made it this far without a lawyer, you can use that fact to your advantage. You can negotiate with the insurance company as an unrepresented party with the knowledge that, at any time, you can hire a lawyer to take over the case. Thus, for example, if the company offers you $5,000 to settle the case, you can advise the company that you will be retaining the services of an experienced P. I. attorney if they won't increase their offer. That may well get the offer up to the point where you are comfortable settling the case.

It gets even better. Once you have obtained the "absolute top offer" from the insurance company, you can then go out shopping for a lawyer. Tell the lawyers you interview about the status of your settlement negotiations. Offer to pay them a percentage of any amount they can negotiate above and beyond the best offer you got from the company yourself. You keep 100% of whatever you alone negotiated. This will be irresistible to many lawyers. There is little doubt that with a very small amount of work, the lawyer will be able to substantially increase the offer. If the lawyer is known in the community as a competent P.I. specialist, the fact of his or her involvement in the case will immediately increase its settlement value. Everybody wins here, except of course for the "poor" insurance company, which wishes you'd never read this book.

HANDLING YOUR LAWSUIT WITHOUT A LAWYER

If the liability for the accident is disputed, it is unlikely that you will be able to negotiate a good settlement without filing lawsuit papers with the court. In most cases you should get a lawyer to do this. But if your case can be handled in small claims court, you cannot find a lawyer to handle your case, or you insist on doing it yourself, here's some guidance.

SMALL CLAIMS COURT

In every state there is a special court for handling small claims. Typically the limit on awards in such a court is between $1,000 and $5,000. Such courts usually have rules that allow a non-lawyer to present a case easily, without the usual court formalities.

If your damages are within the limit of your small claims court you can have a judge decide the merits of your claim. If your claim is above the limits of small claims court you can still file if you are willing to accept the limit. For example, if your damages are $4,000 and your court's limit is $3,000, you can sue in small claims court if you will be happy with $3,000.

On the following page is a list of small claims court limits as of the time of the writing of this book. Since these limits can change you should call your court for current information.

Alabama	$1,500	Montana	$3,000
Alaska	$5,000	Nebraska	$1,800
Arizona	$1,500	Nevada	$3,500
Arkansas	$3,000	New Hampshire	$2,500
California	$5,000	New Jersey	$1,500
Colorado	$3,500	New Mexico	$5,000
Connecticut	$2,000	New York	$3,000
Delaware	$5,000	North Carolina	$3,000
D. C.	$2,000	North Dakota	$3,000
Florida	$5,000	Ohio	$2,000
Georgia	$5,000	Oklahoma	$2,500
Hawaii	$3,500	Oregon	$2,500
Idaho	$3,000	Pennsylvania	$8,000*
Illinois	$2,500	Rhode Island	$1,500
Indiana	$3,000	South Carolina	$2,500
Iowa	$4,000	South Dakota	$4,000
Kansas	$1,800	Tennessee	$10,000*
Kentucky	$1,500	Texas	$5,000
Louisiana	$2,000	Utah	$5,000
Maine	$3,000	Vermont	$3,500
Maryland	$2,500	Virginia	$10,000*
Massachusetts	$2,000	Washington	$2,500
Michigan	$1,750	West Virginia	$3,000
Minnesota	$7,500	Wisconsin	$4,000
Mississippi	$1,000	Wyoming	$2,000*
Missouri	$1,500		

*Pennsylvania—$10,000 in Philadelphia; Tennessee—$15,000 if county has over 700,000 residents; Virginia—up to $10,000 varies by county; Wyoming—$7,000 for County Court.

One danger of filing a suit in small claims court is that the other side may hire a lawyer and countersue you for more than the limit in small claims court. Then you will have to hire a lawyer to defend you in a higher court. In a medical malpractice suit it is unlikely that the doctor could countersue (unless you didn't pay the bill), but in an auto accident where the fault is disputed you could easily end up being liable for more than the amount for which you sued. Consider getting a lawyer to review your case before filing such a suit.

The procedures and options in small claims court can take an entire book to explain and there are many good books on the subject that you can find in public libraries, law libraries, and bookstores. You should read one before going to court.

FORMAL
COURT

If your claim is much greater than the limit in small claims court, you might consider filing suit in your regular court system. Unless you have some legal training or can devote considerable time to learning all the court procedures, this is not a good idea. Court rules are strict, and your case can be lost because of a minor mistake. If the other side has a lawyer, he or she will be looking at your every move for an error that will doom your case. If you feel you cannot afford to give a third of your claim to an attorney, try to get a good offer from the other side and then seek out an attorney who will only take a percentage of what he or she gains for you over the last offer.

If you still insist upon going to formal court by yourself, you should go to a law library and read a good book on civil procedure in your state. The best books are often put out by bar association continuing legal education (CLE) offices and are used by lawyers who want to learn procedure. Most law libraries do not allow books to circulate, so plan to spend some time there. Bring plenty of change for the copy machine, too. If you are really serious you might be able to buy a copy of the CLE book from the state bar association. If they won't sell it to you, try a law school bookstore.

Chapters 7 through 9 of this book provide an outline of how a personal injury case progresses through court. It will guide you through the aspects of civil procedure that are most important to your case.

The Appendix of this book contains two forms for lawsuit complaints that I use in personal injury cases. These are samples only, and the correct form for your court may be somewhat different, but something similar should work wherever you file. To find a more exact version of what is proper in your state you can locate a file of similar lawsuits filed by a lawyer in your local court. You should have no trouble viewing someone else's file since they are public records. The important thing is to find the right type of case. This is easiest to do if your court clerk has an index of cases that lists the type of case. Look for personal injury cases and then find one similar to your own. Form 12 is a sample complaint for use for a car accident. Form 13 is a sample complaint for fall down accidents.

It is important that your lawsuit papers be properly filed and properly delivered to the defendant. You should contact the court to find out the cost for filing the lawsuit, the number of copies that have to be filed, etc.

SERVICE OF PROCESS

You need to be very careful with "service of process." Service of process is the legal terminology for delivering the lawsuit papers to the defendant. In some jurisdictions only service by a sheriff is proper. If you make a mistake here, it can be fatal to your case. Don't be afraid to ask lots of questions. If one person at the court won't help you, find someone who will. While court personnel cannot give legal advice, they can usually provide procedural guidance. Court employees in some areas are notorious for not caring how helpful they are, so take extra care to ensure that you get good advice. You might also go to your local law library for forms and books on filing and serving papers. Alternatively, you can retain an attorney on an hourly basis to consult with about these technical, but important legal matters. Just an hour or so of skilled legal help may be all you need.

Once you have successfully filed and served the suit papers, one of many things can happen. The insurance company may then be ready to settle the case. Your skill thus far may have impressed the company enough to make them want to buy their peace. Or perhaps the company will turn its lawyers loose on you. These lawyers may file motions with the court regarding some supposed legal problem with the complaint. If this happens, it really may be time to throw in the towel and hire a lawyer. It would be very hard to fight off these legal motions without proper advice.

Once the motions are decided, the case moves into the "discovery" phase. See Chapter 8 for a detailed discussion of that important process. Form 16 is a sample set of Interrogatories for a typical car accident case. "Interrogatories" are simply questions that pertain to your lawsuit. For fall down accidents, see Form 17. For a sample Request for Production of Documents, see Form 14. These items should help you prepare your own Interrogatories and Request for Production. Unless you submit these discovery requests to the insurance company attorney, he or she won't have to turn over the information in his or her file. Believe me, you need to get this information, so don't wait. Send Interrogatories and a Request for Production of Documents to the opposing lawyer on the very day that he or she enters his or her appearance on behalf of the insurance company. If the attorney won't voluntarily turn this information over, you will have to file a discovery motion in order to get the court's assistance. The form discovery motions take varies from court to court, so you will have to do some research. Form 18 is a sample Motion to Compel Discovery, and Form 19 is a sample Order for Discovery.

DEPOSITIONS

After the documents have been exchanged and all the Interrogatories answered, the case will move into the most important part of the discovery phase: depositions. In a deposition a party or other witness is put under oath and asked a series of questions by one of the attorneys. Form 11 is a list of questions you can expect at your deposition. Chapter 8 gives you a detailed list of rules for your deposition. If you are representing yourself you've got an additional task. You need to take the defendant's deposition. In a car accident case, this is the person who hit you. In a fall down case, this is the owner of the home where you fell or the store manager of the business where you were hurt. Or it can be any other witness the insurance company has to testify on its behalf at the trial. You need to know what these people will say at trial. You're at a severe disadvantage if you submit to a deposition without taking one or more yourself.

It is during depositions that your inexperience may be most damaging. The insurance company's lawyer may try to take advantage of you. In fact, you can pretty much count on that. You need to be as familiar as possible with the rules for taking depositions in your jurisdiction. And once you're familiar with those rules, stick to your guns. Don't let the attorney intimidate you. He or she will try things he or she wouldn't dream of doing in court at depositions because no judges or juries are present.

During the trial, your opponent's lawyer, if he or she has one, will try to appear to be fair. Juries hate lawyers who try to take advantage of unrepresented litigants. But in the deposition room, the action takes place in relative privacy. You'll probably be in the opposing lawyer's conference room with only his or her stenographer present to record the testimony. The lawyer will be on his home ground and you'll be in unfamiliar territory. This can be very intimidating, but there is hope. You need to find out in advance which judge is in charge of discovery disputes. Then, when a problem arises during the deposition, you can threaten to call the judge. This will impress the defense lawyer greatly. He or she will very much fear having a judge come down on him or her for having tried to take advantage of an unrepresented plaintiff.

Once the depositions are done, there is nothing left to do but prepare for trial. The better your preparation and the more the insurance company understands that you are prepared, the easier it will be settle the case for a fair amount of money. Many cases settle on the day of trial or shortly before. You should prepare as if the case will not settle, and then be delighted if by chance it does. You can't count on a last-minute settlement. Preparation is the key.

I suggest that you watch a trial or two before your case goes to court. You'll need to find a case that is similar to yours to get the maximum benefit from watching. Ask if you can see the court "docket." This lists cases and the courtrooms in which they will be heard. Hopefully the docket will also list the type of case. You will learn many helpful things by watching experienced attorneys try a personal injury case. Also, please review Chapter 9 of this book carefully, where you will find a step-by-step analysis of the trial of a personal injury lawsuit.

PROVING YOUR CASE

You must prove every aspect of a negligence case to be entitled to an award in your favor. These aspects include negligence (carelessness), causation and damages. Thus, you must prove that the defendant's behavior was careless or in some way unreasonable, that his or her behavior caused you to be injured and, of course, you must prove the extent of your damages. With regard to negligence, if the defendant rear-ended you, negligence is clear. Or if you trip over the defendant's broken and deteriorated sidewalk, the defendant's negligence should be no problem to prove. In the latter case, however, your own carelessness (comparative negligence) in tripping over an obvious defect may limit your claim. See Chapter 9 for a discussion of comparative negligence. You must always prove that the defendant's behavior caused your injury. If you had a pre-existing injury or were injured again shortly after the accident, the defense lawyer will try to prove that his or her client's negligence was not the primary cause of your injuries. Or if x-rays show arthritis, he or she may argue that your pain and suffering is simply due to old age rather than to the accident. The method for proving a personal injury case varies from court to court. Also, whether your case is heard by a judge, jury or some other less formal panel will affect how you have to prove your case. For example, if your case is a jury or judge trial, you probably will have to offer your doctor's spoken testimony into evidence. If your case is an arbitration, it may be possible to prove your damages simply by offering his or her medical reports. See Chapter 7 for a discussion of the types of trials.

Acting as your own lawyer during the trial has certain advantages. You will be viewed by both the jury and the judge with special sympathy because you are unrepresented. The technical rules of court will probably be relaxed for you since you can't fairly be expected to have the sophistication of a trial lawyer. Yet the rules can only be bent so far.

For example, everyone has heard of "hearsay." The hearsay doctrine prevents a witness from testifying about what another person said. There are exceptions to this rule that are too numerous and complicated to discuss here. If your case hinges on inadmissible hearsay and you are unaware of the rule against its admission, you will lose your case no matter how much sympathy the judge has for you. I therefore suggest that, before you go to court, you hire a lawyer on an hourly basis, or for some percentage of the final award, to go through the evidence with you to be sure you don't make any fatal mistakes.

The Personal Injury Attorney and You 3

Finding a Personal Injury Attorney

If you decide to hire a personal injury attorney, you must find an attorney you can trust. You should also be sure that he or she has some experience.

RECOMMENDATIONS

The very best way to find a good personal injury lawyer is by asking close friends or family members for recommendations. But be sure that the recommendation is to an attorney who specializes in personal injury litigation. The days when one lawyer can help you with all of your legal problems are over. Most lawyers today specialize in one or two areas and refer all other cases to other attorneys. There are so many competent personal injury attorneys out there that it is an absolute mistake to retain anyone but a specialist.

BAR ASSOCIATION

You can also check with your local bar association to find out if the lawyer you are considering has a good reputation. Some bar associations are not permitted to recommend attorneys. They must be neutral. If you cannot find the right lawyer through the recommendation of a friend or family member or through a bar association, you might get really creative and do your own research. You must be willing to take some time and make a considerable effort if you wish to take this route, but I think it is well worth it.

LEGAL JOURNALS

I suggest that you consult a legal journal in your area that reviews the results of personal injury cases. You can find these publications in your local law library or through the bar association. This review will provide you with the facts of many cases, the names of the lawyers and the outcome. Perhaps you will find a case similar to yours that turned out favorably for the plaintiff. If so, you can contact the plaintiff's lawyer. One of the first questions he or she will ask you is how you found him or her. You can bet he or she will be quite impressed with your ingenuity in locating him or her this way.

REFERRALS

Even if he or she cannot represent you, your plaintiff's lawyer contact may be able to refer you to someone who can. Lawyers generally receive referral fees when they send clients to one another. At the end of your case, the referring attorney may receive as much as one third of the attorney fees simply for making a phone call to another lawyer. Nice work if you can get it. The downside to this is that the lawyer who actually does the work does not receive a full fee. This could reduce his or her incentive to work as hard on the file as if he or she got to keep the whole fee. It is unethical for an attorney to put less effort into a case for this reason. But human nature dictates that sometimes this will be the unfortunate result of the referral fee system.

The up side is that you will end up with a personal injury specialist. The referring attorney is doubly motivated to find the best lawyer for you. Not only is he or she ethically bound to refer you to someone who will zealously pursue your case, he or she has a financial incentive to find someone who will obtain a maximum settlement or verdict in the least possible amount of time.

Note that it is illegal for lawyers to pay referral fees to non-lawyers. This is to discourage "ambulance chasing." If you insist on receiving such a fee, you will alienate your attorney, assuming he or she practices law ethically. If he or she offers you a fee for sending him or her cases, find a new lawyer.

The worst way to pick a lawyer is by the recommendation of someone you first meet at the accident scene. This nation's big cities are filled with "ambulance chasers" who magically appear at accident scenes ready to advise the vulnerable accident victim. These vultures are on the payroll of unethical lawyers who make their living off of the assembly line handling of vast numbers of personal injury cases, some real and some faked, or at least exaggerated. You should not trust your important rights to someone who practices the great profession of law in an unethical and unscrupulous way.

ADVERTISEMENTS   Another questionable way to find an attorney is through an advertisement. The Yellow Pages are filled with the ads of P. I. lawyers, some of whom are extremely competent and some of whom are unscrupulous ambulance chasers. If you must choose a lawyer from an ad, interview several and then investigate the credentials of those you like. Your state or city bar association maintains disciplinary files that can help you to steer clear of unethical practitioners. These files are not always open to the public.

P. I. lawyers almost never charge for the initial consultation. You can interview as many as you like before you sign a fee agreement. However, it is a bad idea to wait too long before selecting one. A prompt investigation by your lawyer may be crucial to your case. So if you're comfortable with the first lawyer you meet, you can sign a fee agreement and let him or her begin the investigation. If you sign a fee agreement but then change your mind, you can still fire the first lawyer and hire a new one. The first lawyer is required to turn your file over to the new lawyer. The lawyers will divide one attorney's fee. You should not have to pay extra for changing lawyers.

Treat your selection of a personal injury lawyer the way you would any matter of importance in your life. Your choice of a lawyer may make the difference between years of uncertainty and stress, and a rapid, successful and not unpleasant experience. Some people actually even enjoy their exposure to this legal process.

THE INITIAL CONSULTATION

The initial consultation is similar to meeting for the first time with a doctor. The doctor takes your medical history; the lawyer reviews your legal history. The two-way communication between lawyer and client is the crucial first step in achieving a successful outcome.

Before the appointment, try to write down the details of the accident. Your notes, and Forms 1 or 2 and Form 10 from this book, will help you to provide your lawyer with complete and thorough information. Bring your notes, all of your insurance papers, your doctor's name and address as well as any discharge forms you received from the hospital. If you have photographs of your car, the accident scene, or your injuries, bring them as well. Your attorney will very much appreciate your interest in the case. If the photographs are of good quality, it may not be necessary for your lawyer to go to the expense of having professional photos taken. This will save you a significant amount of money, since litigation costs are ultimately the client's responsibility.

The attorney will ask you to sign medical authorizations and a fee agreement if he or she wants to pursue the case. The medical authorization allows the lawyer to collect your medical records. See Form 5 in the Appendix for a sample medical authorization. Immediately after the initial meeting, an attorney will often send a "new client letter." See Form 4 for a sample of this type of letter.

Many of your questions about the P. I. process can be answered during the initial consultation. However, not all questions can be answered at that time with any degree of certainty. For example, there is no way for the lawyer to know at the initial meeting what the case is "worth," how long before it will settle, whether you will have to go to court, etc. More questions will arise in your mind in the weeks and months to come. You should not hesitate to call your lawyer for answers. That's why he or she is there.

During the initial consultation, tell the lawyer that you want to receive copies of all letters he or she sends out on your behalf. Many lawyers make this a practice for several reasons. First of all, they feel they have an ethical obligation to keep their clients informed about their cases. But further, an informed client is often a very helpful client. Clients who take an active interest in their case provide important details that might otherwise be overlooked. They can also correct mistakes made by the lawyer or his or her staff. While the lawyer has the legal expertise, no one is more aware of the factual background of the case than the client. The team approach helps the client feel involved and respected, and it helps the lawyer do a good job for the client.

THE ATTORNEY'S FEE AGREEMENT

Personal injury lawyers usually use what are known as contingent fee agreements, that is, agreements that base the attorney's fee on a percentage of the overall settlement. The lawyer's fee is contingent upon settlement of the case. These agreements have been called "the key to the courthouse" for many people, since the client usually does not have to pay any up-front money to the lawyer.

Detractors feel that contingent fee agreements promote litigation. There is no doubt that more people sue because of these agreements. Many countries do not allow such agreements, and have much less litigation. However, others feel the empowerment they provide to the average citizen, and the accountability they force upon big business, justify their use. Contingent fee agreements are the great equalizer. They allow both the indigent and the middle class to engage in expensive litigation to recover for losses. The P. I. lawyer is a modern day Robin Hood of sorts. They take from the rich and give to the poor. Of course, Robin Hood never took a large chunk for himself.

The typical contingent fee agreement calls for the client to receive two-thirds of the settlement, with the balance of one-third going to the lawyer. These agreements give the attorney a stake, or ownership interest, in the litigation. The lawyer gambles that the outcome of the case justifies the time expenditure, monetary investment and stress involved.

You should not hesitate to try to negotiate a better deal with your lawyer. Especially if you have a good case, your lawyer will be willing to reduce his or her fee if he or she thinks you'll shop for a more favorable arrangement. For example, you could offer 20% if the case settles before a suit is filed, 25% if a suit must be filed and 33% if a trial is necessary.

This country, unfortunately, is filled with lawyers, including personal injury lawyers. There are lots of bad P. I. lawyers, and there are many dishonest, unscrupulous ones, too. But there are also many skilled, honest, and energetic personal injury lawyers to choose from. It's a client's market and you should take advantage of that fact. If you feel that the fee your lawyer wants to charge to handle your case is too high, let him or her know that you would like to negotiate a fee arrangement which will result in you receiving a larger part of the settlement proceeds. It can't hurt to ask.

Your lawyer may not like the fact that you are sophisticated enough to ask, but he or she will respect it. If he or she doesn't like it, you can always find another lawyer. P. I. lawyers, at least average ones, are "a dime a dozen." If you have a good case, you are in the driver's seat, so to speak. You are free to take your case and leave if you are not satisfied with the terms the lawyer offers. You will be amazed at how willing he or she will be to re-negotiate if he or she senses that you are ready to head for the door.

At the same time, the fee agreement the lawyer is willing to offer you is not the most important factor in choosing a lawyer. It is more important that you choose a lawyer who is honest, hard working and experienced in personal injury work. If you shop around for the best possible fee agreement, you may find a bad lawyer who will outbid the rest. Be sure you know what you are getting into before you sign on the dotted line. Again, speak to friends you trust or consult your local bar association before retaining a lawyer.

There is an element of uncertainty for the lawyer with contingent fee cases. The lawyer assumes the risk that there may be no or little recovery after years of work and thousands of dollars of the attorney's own money invested in the costs of litigation. Because of this risk, it is fair that personal injury lawyers sometimes earn more on a contingent fee case than if they were paid hourly.

Lawyers usually bill on an hourly basis for cases that do not involve personal injuries. The insurance company's lawyer, in defending against the personal injury claim, bills the company in this manner. Hourly rates of $150 or more have become commonplace. Lawyers who work on an hourly basis are often criticized for putting in unnecessary time on the case. This is called "padding" the time sheet. Attorneys who work with contingency fees are not subject to this criticism, since more time spent on the case does not necessarily translate into higher attorney fees. In fact, the criticism is just the opposite. The clients of P. I. lawyers frequently complain that they can't reach their attorney. The lawyer may avoid the client because the lawyer can't bill the time and may feel that client contact is unnecessary or a nuisance.

While you should not stand for being ignored by your lawyer, keep in mind that he or she cannot make progress on your case or those of other clients if he or she is on the phone all day answering clients' questions. If you have a question about your case, ask your lawyer's secretary or paralegal. Often he or she can provide the right answer just as easily as the lawyer.

Contingent fee agreements motivate the lawyer to work efficiently. Since the lawyer cannot bill hourly, he or she hopes to settle the case for as much as possible as soon as possible. The lawyer doesn't get paid until the conclusion of the case. This arrangement, at least theoretically, rewards diligence and hard work. It's pure capitalism. It works for trial lawyers and it works for their clients. When big business and the insurance industry complain about contingent fee agreements, they are thinking only of their self-interest.

One of the most attractive aspects of contingent fee agreements is that the client owes the lawyer nothing if the case is not won. This should provide the lawyer with strong motivation to aggressively handle the case in order to obtain a large and prompt settlement.

You should insist on receiving a copy of the fee agreement for your records. Form 3 in the Appendix is a sample contingent fee agreement.

As explained in the last chapter under THE BEST OF BOTH WORLDS, be sure that if you are paying the lawyer a percentage, it is only a percentage of what he or she obtains for you. If the insurance company has already offered you $50,000, you should only pay a fee on any additional amount the lawyer negotiates for you.

BEWARE OF "COSTS"

In addition to the lawyer's fee, there will be other costs involved in pursuing your case. These include court filing fees, court reporter fees, expert witness fees, and many things you would never imagine. In major litigation cases the costs amount to hundreds of thousands, or even millions, of dollars.

Unless the case is extremely difficult, the P. I. lawyer puts up the costs required to investigate the case, file the legal papers, etc. These are repaid to the lawyer at the successful conclusion of the case. In auto accidents and fall down cases, the lawyer almost always pays for these costs up front. In medical malpractice cases, unless the liability seems clear and the injuries are severe, the client may be asked to pay the cost of gathering the medical records and having them reviewed. This varies from case to case and from lawyer to lawyer.

How these fees are paid should be spelled out clearly in the fee agreement. One major issue is whether the costs come out of the client's share of the proceeds or if they are taken out before the proceeds are split. Because the costs can be extremely high, how this is calculated can make a big difference in the outcome.

For example, consider a $100,000 award where the costs are $20,000 and the lawyer gets a fee of 33.3%. If the costs come out before the balance is split the lawyer will get $26,666 and the client $53,334. If the costs all come out of the plaintiff's share, the lawyer will get $33,333 and the client $46,667. This is a difference of $6,667.

You should insist that the costs be taken out of any award first, before the attorney takes his or her percentage. Otherwise you will end up with a much smaller percentage of the net proceeds than you thought.

DISSATISFACTION WITH ATTORNEYS

"The first thing we do, let's kill all the lawyers." Those words, first uttered hundreds of years ago by one of Shakespeare's characters, still reflect the feelings of a large segment of the population. The complaint that is most commonly heard is that the lawyer doesn't communicate properly with the client, that telephone messages are not returned promptly, if ever. The lawyer may well be doing a satisfactory job for the client, but if communications break down, the client can be left feeling powerless, irritated, and dissatisfied.

The solution to this problem lies in letting your lawyer know in clear and certain terms that you are unhappy. A strongly worded letter, sent perhaps by certified mail, will get the lawyer's attention and probably assure a prompt phone call. The letter should express your specific complaints and your desire to hire a new attorney if the necessary steps are not promptly taken. If a satisfactory response is not forthcoming, it may be time to seek out the assistance of another attorney.

CHANGING LAWYERS

Most clients are reluctant to fire one attorney and hire another one. The client might be afraid to hurt the lawyer's feelings by rejecting him or her in this way, or the client may believe that a double attorney's fee will have to be paid if a second lawyer is brought into the picture. This is not the way it works in personal injury cases. The client should not be charged one extra dime when he or she fires one lawyer and hires another. The two lawyers will work out an arrangement in which they split one attorney's fee.

Lawyers are often hesitant about taking a case that another lawyer has been handling. There are many valid reasons for this. The client may simply have unreasonable expectations about the case and the second lawyer may end up having to deal with the first lawyer's headaches. The second lawyer may fear that some day the first lawyer may exact revenge for losing the client, or the second lawyer may simply feel that the case cannot be profitably handled since the fee has to be split with the first lawyer. Nevertheless, it is worth checking into changing attorneys if, after making your dissatisfaction known, you are still dissatisfied with your lawyer's performance.

Lawyers frequently receive telephone calls from individuals complaining about the lawyer currently handling their personal injury case. Many of these calls involve requests to evaluate the strategy, or lack thereof, of the caller's current attorney. When a lawyer receives this type of call, he or she may respond in a way that is somewhat unsatisfactory to the caller. The lawyer doesn't mean to be evasive, but the request for this kind of information places him or her in a very bad position for several reasons. First of all, he or she does not have access to the caller's file and is in no position at all to evaluate the other attorney's strategy.

Requests for information about your file should be directed to your present attorney. Your attorney has the obligation to communicate with you in a timely and courteous fashion and to respond to all reasonable requests for information. Again, if your attorney is not responsive, you should send a certified letter requesting the information you seek. This is sure to get your attorney's attention.

Further, you can be sure that your attorney will very much resent being second-guessed by an outside attorney who has only one side of the story. Most attorneys prefer not to advise a client at this stage that his or her current attorney is handling the case improperly. If they were to provide such advice, they would open themselves up to lawsuits or complaints to the disciplinary board by the first attorney. Please don't expect a lawyer to subject himself or herself to that risk.

Worse yet, because the second lawyer is operating with only one side of the story and very incomplete information, any advice he or she might give would very likely be unsatisfactory, and perhaps completely erroneous. This might subject the lawyer to a later lawsuit by the client for legal malpractice.

Thus, if an attorney politely refuses your request for an evaluation of a case another attorney is handling, there may be solid reasons for the refusal.

Occasionally you can find an attorney who will inform your attorney that you are concerned and ask if he or she can help clarify the present situation. If you do not mind paying this other attorney to act as a buffer for you, a simple phone call may help alleviate your fears that your case is being mishandled. If you have a friend or relative who is an attorney, but not a personal injury attorney, he or she may be able to talk lawyer-to-lawyer with your attorney and express your concerns without making the attorney fear he or she will lose the case.

If all attempts at resolving the problem with your lawyer fail, you should seek out a new attorney. You have the right to expect competent representation and courteous treatment. You deserve the same level of representation that the insurance company expects from its lawyers.

If you decide to change attorneys, you must take certain steps to assure a smooth transition. First, the new lawyer communicates with the old lawyer that you desire the change. The new lawyer may ask you to write to the old lawyer to advise him or her to turn your file over. The lawyers then must work out financial arrangements so that everyone's interests are protected. The old lawyer is entitled to be reimbursed for the costs he or she has spent on the case. And he or she is also entitled to be paid for his or her time, although that payment generally comes at the end of the case.

The second lawyer hopes to review the file as soon as possible in order to determine if he or she indeed wishes to represent the client. If it looks like the case can profitably be pursued, the second lawyer will take the case over. The case needs to be quite attractive since the lawyers have to split the fee. If there's "not enough to go around," the second lawyer may make a business judgment that he or she is not interested in taking the case. That leaves the client with an upset first lawyer and a case in legal limbo. The client could be left with no choice but to go lawyer shopping. That's the risk you run when you fire your lawyer, and that's why it pays to select a good one on the first go round.

Insurance companies react in various ways to a change in lawyers. They may view the switch as a sign that the case or the client is a problem from your lawyer's perspective. This can result in increased reluctance to settle and a stepped-up investigation into the merits of the case. Another possibility is that the new lawyer will breathe needed energy into the case, causing the insurance company to start thinking seriously of settlement. The reputation and ability of the new lawyer are key to the insurance company's reaction to a switch in representation.

There is one thing you must avoid doing if you are dissatisfied with your lawyer. You must under no circumstances contact the insurance company yourself. I have heard of clients who, out of distrust for their lawyer, contacted the insurance firm to find out what was actually going on with their case. Perhaps the client simply didn't believe the lawyer's explanation concerning a delay in the settlement of the case.

Insurance companies operate out of a "where there's smoke there's fire" mindset. If you contact the insurance company yourself, this will signify to the insurance company that something is wrong somewhere, either with you, your lawyer, or both. Once the insurance company smells smoke it will suspect that there is a problem with you or your case. The chances for a quick settlement will immediately fly out the window.

Then, instead of securing a quick settlement, your lawyer will probably have to file the lawsuit and prepare to engage in extended and expensive discovery. (See Chapter 8 for more on discovery.) The insurance company will not only demand your deposition, but it will also undoubtedly subpoena every record that conceivably can provide it with information to use against you. It may subpoena your doctor's records, your employment records, and maybe even your school records. Only after all this discovery, if it turns out that, despite the "smoke," there was no fire, will settlement discussions resume. Even worse, the insurance company's lawyers often find something during discovery that can severely damage your case. If that happens, the settlement value of your case drops and the case may have to go to trial. The bottom line here is that you should never contact the insurance company directly. You should let your lawyer handle all contacts with that company.

KEEPING YOUR LAWYER ON HIS OR HER TOES

It is your job to be very actively involved with your case from the day of the accident or event, until the check clears the bank. That is the best way to ensure that your lawyer does his or her job properly. Many personal injury attorneys are overworked or are simply too lazy to do the job right without prompting. Everyone has heard that "the squeaky wheel gets the grease." Nowhere is this truism more important than in personal injury litigation.

FIRMS Especially if you have entrusted your case to one of the larger personal injury firms, your situation may be pushed onto an associate who has nothing financially to gain by handling your case aggressively. The famous partner who is known for several multi-million dollar jury verdicts may simply not have the time for your little case. Don't be surprised if some fresh-faced 24-year-old gets handed your file. Now don't get me wrong. Many young lawyers are filled with energy for effective battle with the insurance companies. But many are handling a hundred or more other files, and yours may be placed on a very slow assembly line. They may be inexperienced, stressed out and unprepared to handle your case properly.

Worse, the associate may have no financial stake in your case. The arrangements vary from firm to firm, but at the vast majority, the only lawyer who has a financial interest in your case is the one who brought the case into the firm. The lowly associate who actually ends up processing the case is undoubtedly on straight salary. His or her financial incentive is to turn over his or her cases with the least bother to him or her, even if this means settling the case for less than it's worth. If, however, you retain a solo practitioner or small partnership, the lawyer who handles your case will actually receive the attorney's fees earned on the case. Nothing motivates like a financial incentive. Even though lawyers are ethically bound to zealously represent the interests of all their clients, human nature should tell you that you will do best if your lawyer has something to gain by prosecuting your case aggressively and forcefully.

YOUR PART   Staying active throughout the process is important regardless of the lawyer you retain. If your case has been shuffled off to an associate, your involvement is especially critical. You should insist on receiving copies of all correspondence your lawyer sends out on your behalf. You can even ask for copies of all letters from the insurance company and its lawyers. You should also review your medical records for accuracy. The only way you can know for sure that your lawyer is being straight with you is if you have access to the file. Also, since the lawyer knows you are keeping close tabs on your case, he or she will be sure not to put it on the "back burner." In other words, he or she will know that, unless he or she stays very active, you will be contacting him or her with difficult questions. It is your right to know what is going on at all times with your case. It is also your right to have a lawyer who will aggressively pursue a rapid and fair settlement of your case. Do not accept anything less. The squeaky wheel does indeed get the grease.

I suggest that you wait a week or so after the initial interview with the lawyer before you call to find out how things are going. You will want to know if witnesses have been contacted, if a request for the police report has been made, etc. You can then follow up a couple weeks later and then perhaps once a month after that. Of course if specific questions come up, you should feel free to call anytime.

THE PROBLEM CLIENT

But you don't want to turn into a "problem client." Problem clients call every other day, often just to talk. Problem clients may call to complain about everything that's wrong in their life. Your lawyer is not there to hold your hand or to become your social companion. Most lawyers are simply too busy for that. Organize your thoughts before you make the call so that you can make your points and ask your questions clearly and concisely. Lawyers are used to processing information quickly and directly. If you chatter endlessly in a disorganized fashion, your lawyer may wish to terminate the conversation as soon as possible. Trial lawyering can be a very stressful way to make a living. If your phone calls add to this stress, your lawyer may dread your calls. If prematurely terminated calls cause your attorney to miss out on useful information, your case will suffer. Your lawyer will resent the fact that he or she has to waste a lot of time on activities that do nothing to further your case. Human nature may cause your lawyer to recommend settlement of your case for less than it's worth so that he or she can close your file and rid himself or herself of a problem client. Treat your lawyer with the respect and courtesy you would like to be treated with, and you will ensure the best possible result.

SETTLEMENT PACKAGE

When your medical treatment is completed, let your lawyer know. Insist that he or she immediately finish the process of gathering your records and organizing them into a settlement package. A settlement package is a collection of your medical bills and reports, photographs, and expert witness reports. Expert witnesses can be economists retained to determine your economic losses, vocational specialists who help determine the jobs available for injured plaintiffs who can no longer do their old job, etc. Assuming the cooperation of your doctors, the settlement package should be on its way to the insurance company within a month after you finish your treatment. If it isn't, find out why. The first offer of settlement should be made within 3 weeks after the settlement package is sent. If it isn't, find out why. If the case isn't settled within 6 weeks after the package is sent, find out why. If the case doesn't settle, insist that your lawyer immediately prepare the lawsuit papers. This should take no more than an hour to complete. These papers should be in your hands within a week. The suit should be filed by the time another week passes. But these things will happen only if your lawyer is on his or her toes. And most lawyers need prompting from their clients to stay there. Keeping tabs on the progress of your case does not make you a problem client, just an actively concerned one. Your lawyer should appreciate your interest.

DISCOVERY

Even after the suit is filed, you need to stay active. Be sure your lawyer is aggressively pursuing discovery. (See Chapter 8 for more on discovery.) When it comes time to respond to the other lawyer's discovery requests, it is very important that you work closely with your lawyer. Be sure that the information he or she provides to the other lawyer is accurate. If it is not, you are the one the other lawyer will crucify at trial, not your lawyer.

DOUBLE CHECKING

It is very easy for an overworked or lazy lawyer to get it wrong. It is up to you to double check the information to be provided to the other side. You may feel that your lawyer is being paid handsomely to do the job right. You may resent having to help him or her do this job. If so, feel free to trust that your lawyer will get it right. But don't complain when mistakes are made. It is much better and easier to catch errors before they become problems. Try to think of your case as a challenging game to succeed at, rather than a difficult job to avoid doing. You can think of yourself and your lawyer as partners, with you having special knowledge of the facts and your lawyer having special knowledge of the law. Your case is an opportunity to learn and grow, not just to make money.

DEPOSITIONS
AND TRIAL
TESTIMONY

The most important phases of a personal injury case are depositions (Chapter 8) and the trial (Chapter 9). Preparation is key. Be sure your lawyer knows that you expect him or her to take all the time needed with you to ensure that no mistakes are made. If your case is an average personal injury matter, your deposition will probably last about an hour and a half. Your lawyer should spend at least an hour with you prior to the deposition getting you ready for it. Later you will also need to prepare for your trial testimony. Again you should spend at least an hour with your lawyer just before the trial in preparation. If the young lawyer assigned to your case resists taking the time to prepare you, you may be in big trouble. Call the partner who attracted you to the firm in the first place and find out why you are not being given an adequate preparation session. Preparation for testimony is a very important part of your case. If you are being neglected, don't worry about ruffling the feathers of the associate handling the case. Call the partner and complain.

THE VARIOUS KINDS OF INJURY CASES 4

There are many different kinds of injury cases. These cases are sometimes referred to as "tort" cases. The word "tort" comes from the French word meaning "wrong." The wrongdoer is known as the tortfeasor. Sometimes injury cases are called "negligence" cases. "Negligence" is defined in injury law as the failure to exercise the care for the safety of another that the ordinary prudent person would use under similar circumstances. "Negligence" is an inadequate label, since some types of injury cases involve more than mere negligence. An example would be an injury caused intentionally, like an assault. For simplicity and completeness, I refer to all of these matters as "injury cases."

The concept of "fault" runs throughout any examination of injury cases. Fault must be proven before the injured party can obtain a legal remedy or judgment. The concept of "no-fault" refers to a system of payment of lost wages and medical bills resulting from an accident. The system originated to allow quick compensation without the need to fight over who was at fault. Fault need not be proven to collect these benefits, and thus, the term no-fault benefits. Auto accident victims are entitled to no-fault benefits even if they caused the accident.

This chapter will review some of the different types of injury cases.

INJURIES TO CHILDREN

A mother and father's worst nightmare is receiving a call from the hospital informing them that their child has been involved in an accident. While the physical and emotional suffering from such an event can never be set right by money, a lawsuit against the person at fault may be in the child's best interests. Handled properly, this type of case almost always results in fair compensation for the child.

While most people feel sympathy for injured children, don't expect obtaining financial compensation to be simple. In an automobile accident case, for example, the insurance companies typically take the position that the child ran suddenly into the street and that the driver had no chance to react. The insurance companies refer to these cases as "pedestrian dart-out" cases. By labeling it this way, the insurance companies hope to create the impression that there was no way for the driver to avoid the accident. Personal injury lawyers, on the other hand, refer to these kinds of cases as "pedestrian knock down" cases. You can clearly see the image your attorney hopes to create by using that label.

Regardless of what it is called, the best hope for litigation success when a child is hit by a car is a prompt and thorough investigation of the accident scene. The vital factors include the type of neighborhood where the accident happened, the length of time the child was visible to the motorist, and the age of the child. It is important to photograph the scene of the accident shortly after it occurs if the photos will help to prove that the area was one in which children are likely to be present. Nearby playgrounds, schools, or shops that cater to children should be photographed since these put the motorist on notice that cautious driving is required. Traffic signs that warn motorists to watch for children must be photographed for the same reason.

If it can be proven that the child was visible to the motorist for more than a second or two, the chances for success in this litigation are greatly improved. The adult motorist is presumed to have the capacity to take steps to protect the safety of the child, and he or she must take them promptly in order to avoid responsibility on this claim. Children are often presumed incapable of negligence due to their tender years. The younger the child is, the stronger this presumption generally becomes.

Thus, if a 6-year-old is struck by a car, this child will almost certainly receive compensation for injuries suffered in the accident. A 12-year-old has a much weaker presumption of non-negligence than does a 6-year-old. Yet even the 12-year-old is not held to the same standard of care as the adult driver. That's a very good reason why these cases are so easy to win when handled properly.

Similar rules apply to other accidents involving children, such as injuries on a dangerous piece of property or in a playground. The sooner you take pictures of the scene and get information from witnesses about the situation at the time of the accident, the better.

Juries, judges, and arbitration panels have special sympathy for children. They are much more likely to return large awards for children than they are for adults. Many feel that greed is the primary motivation when adults sue for personal injuries. This factor is far less prominent in the minds of jurors, judges, and arbitrators when it is a child who is injured.

In automobile cases, the medical bills resulting from the child's injuries are paid by the parents' automobile insurer. If there is no insurance in the household, the insurance for the driver has to pay these bills.

FALL DOWN ACCIDENTS ("SLIP AND FALLS")

Automobile accidents and fall down cases are the most common types of lawsuit for personal injuries. The legal principles involved with these types of cases differ greatly. Following are the hurdles that must be overcome in order to receive fair compensation for injuries suffered as the result of a fall.

Generally, the most difficult problem involves the question of notice. The injured victim must prove that the defendant either created the hazard that caused the injury, or that the defendant knew or should have known of the hazard long enough before the accident to have removed or repaired it.

For example, when a pedestrian trips on a crack in a sidewalk, the P. I. attorney hopes to find someone who lives in the area who knows that the crack existed for a long time. Or photos may show that the crack was not of recent origin. It is then easy to show that the property owner should have known of it and should have had the crack repaired. The city where the accident happened may also have liability for failure to enforce the municipal requirements that sidewalks be kept in good repair. This is particularly important when the property owner carries no insurance on the property. In this situation, the government may be the only defendant against whom a money judgment can be collected. The city becomes the "deep pocket" or "target" defendant.

The next issue that almost always comes up in these cases is the victim's own failure to be careful. This is called "comparative negligence." (See Chapter 9 for a discussion of comparative negligence.) Defendants argue that the claimant should have seen the hazard and avoided it. While this argument often reduces the total amount of compensation received, it usually does not defeat the claim outright. There may be valid reasons that the hazard was not seen. For example, when a customer in a grocery store slips on grapes, the customer's attention may have been drawn by a catchy advertisement or display put up by the store. This is a reasonable explanation which, if believed, should enable you to receive full compensation.

A thorough and prompt investigation can make all the difference in the outcome of fall down cases. Witness statements must be obtained and photographs of the hazard must be taken. Even short delays can hurt the case since memories fade rapidly and hazards get repaired quickly when injuries occur.

The discussion that follows sets forth the different classifications that some states use to describe fall down accident plaintiffs. Although these exact classifications may not apply in your state, this discussion should at least enlighten you to some degree as to this subject matter. Be sure to consult the law in your own state.

INVITEES

Property owners and their tenants owe the highest duty of care to individuals they invite onto their property. In some states, customers of businesses have the status of "business invitees." The owner of the business is under the duty to protect the business visitor, not only against dangers the owner knows about, but also against those which with reasonable care he or she might discover. The business invitee enters the business' premises with the assurance that the business owner has taken steps for his or her protection and safety while he or she is there. The store customer is entitled to rely upon the business owner's performance of his or her duty to make the premises safe.

LICENSEES

A lesser standard of care is required with respect to "licensees." In states in which that classification is used, a licensee may be defined as a person who may enter or remain on the property only by virtue of the consent of the possessor of that property. For example, social guests are licensees. Even though a social guest is normally invited, he or she is not on the property for business reasons. A person who cuts through a business parking lot to get to another location is also a licensee. A possessor of land is subject to liability to his or her licensees for injuries caused by the possessor's failure to exercise reasonable care for their safety only under certain circumstances. The licensee must show 1) that the possessor should have expected that the licensee would not discover the danger and 2) that the licensee did not know or have reason to know of the danger. Thus, hidden dangers subject the possessor to liability but open dangers do not.

TRESPASSERS

A trespasser is one who enters the land of another without any right to do so, or who goes beyond the rights or privileges which he or she has been granted by license or invitation. As a general rule, the owner or occupier's duty to a trespasser is to refrain from willfully or wantonly injuring the trespasser. However, foreseeable trespassers may, under certain circumstances, be entitled to greater protection. Thus, an "attractive nuisance" such as an unfenced swimming pool may subject the owner to liability if a child from the neighborhood wanders in and drowns. It is foreseeable that this might happen. Thus, the possessor must protect even trespassers from harm in this kind of case.

MEDICAL MALPRACTICE

I receive call after call from people who want to sue their doctors for medical malpractice. Often these individuals seek legal redress for a bad medical result for which there is no legal blame. Probably four out of every five calls I receive involve a claim in which actual medical malpractice cannot be proven or where it makes no economic sense to even try.

CASE VALIDITY Often the calls I receive are spurred by nothing more than hurt feelings. Perhaps the patient simply felt that the doctor treated him or her with disrespect and he or she wishes to get back at the doctor by filing suit. The law does not provide a remedy for hurt feelings and, practically speaking, it makes no economic sense to pursue a medical malpractice case unless the damages are severe and the liability fairly clear. This is because: 1) A large percentage of malpractice cases must actually be tried before a jury before compensation can be obtained; 2) Malpractice cases are extremely expensive to pursue; 3) Malpractice cases are very time consuming; 4) Malpractice cases are stressful for everyone involved; and 5) Malpractice cases are very difficult to win.

Far more medical malpractice lawsuits actually go to court than do other types of injury cases. Doctors, quite naturally, are often extremely offended when they are contacted by medical malpractice attorneys concerning a possible claim. In some states these claims cannot be settled without the doctor's consent. If the case is settled, it shows up like a black mark on the physician's record. Even where the doctor clearly has committed malpractice, he or she may be unwilling to admit it to the other side or even to himself or herself. In sum, doctors tend to be extremely reluctant to settle these kinds of cases without a bitter battle.

COST
Medical malpractice cases are extremely expensive to pursue. Obtaining medical records, having the records reviewed by an expert, getting the expert witness to write a report and then to testify are all very necessary and very costly elements of a malpractice case. The costs can easily run into tens of thousands of dollars. If the case is particularly difficult, the attorney may ask the client to put up at least some of the costs of the suit. If the case is quite strong, the attorney may be willing to front the costs himself or herself.

SYMPATHY FOR DOCTORS
A large number of malpractice cases end in verdicts for the doctor. Jurors tend to sympathize with doctors who get sued. They tend to respect the wisdom and judgment of doctors. The law also makes it very difficult to win this kind of injury case. The law applicable to medical malpractice cases does not require doctors to be perfect or to practice with mathematical precision. The law of Pennsylvania simply requires that physicians employ such reasonable skill and diligence as is ordinarily exercised in that physician's profession. Your state law is probably similar. It has often been said that, "medicine is an art, not a science." As long as that art is practiced in a "reasonable" manner, the doctor is verdict-proof, even if the medical outcome was poor.

Although lawyers may turn away approximately four out of every five medical malpractice calls, most will meet with anyone who sounds as if they have a legitimate claim. If they feel the case has merit, they will obtain the medical records and have them reviewed by an expert. This expert will then make a preliminary determination concerning the allegation of medical malpractice.

If it turns out that there was no malpractice, at least the client comes to feel that his or her concerns have been taken seriously and that there simply is no feasible legal claim. This is a far more satisfactory situation for clients than being simply left to wonder if they or a family member have been wronged by a member of the medical community. Often having his or her concerns taken seriously is all the client really needs in the first place. Perhaps the doctor just didn't take the time to make the patient feel like a human being. Once the client feels that his or her concerns have been respected, he or she is usually ready to move on with his or her life free of the legal system.

NUISANCE VALUE

Attorneys who file medical malpractice lawsuits without thoroughly investigating them first do everyone a disservice. A medical malpractice lawsuit should only be filed after the records are obtained and reviewed by an expert. Some attorneys hope to harass the doctor into a settlement simply by filing the suit. This is called going for "nuisance value." While this might work sometimes with ordinary injury lawsuits, in medical malpractice cases it usually leads to a huge, lengthy, and bitter legal battle with the doctor, his or her insurance company, and his or her lawyer. This lawyer may end up scrambling at the last minute to find a doctor who will support his or her case. The lawyer or client will spend a great deal of time, money, and emotional energy trying to prove a case that possibly should not have been filed in the first place. The client loses, the lawyer loses, the doctor loses, the doctor's insurance company loses, and society loses.

Because malpractice suits are so expensive, time consuming, and bitterly contested, many attorneys do not file suit in a case of this nature unless they feel that the jury will return an award in excess of $75,000. It is simply not worth pursuing smaller claims even if a jury ultimately might find that the doctor committed malpractice.

If you feel you have a medical malpractice claim and have talked to some attorneys and none of them wish to handle your case, it may be because they feel the case cannot be won or because the case is too small. If they all feel your case cannot be won, accept this and get on with your life. Keep in mind that things happen in life that aren't fair and be glad that things are not worse.

PRODUCTS LIABILITY

Products liability law involves injuries resulting from defective products. These are often among the most serious injuries. Products liability cases arise when injuries occur because of a defectively designed, manufactured, repaired, or maintained product. For example, if a company designs automobile airbags that don't inflate properly upon impact, the laws of products liability apply to the injury lawsuits that are filed.

STRICT LIABILITY

The products liability law in your state may have the concept of strict liability. Strict liability involves the assessment of liability on the basis of the defect itself. The law permits liability to be assessed against the defendant on proof that the product was defective.

KEEP THE PRODUCT

If you are injured by a defective product, hold on to the product for dear life. You must have access to the product to have the best chance for success in the lawsuit. If you do not have access to the product, contact a lawyer immediately. Your lawyer can assure that the product is not destroyed. If the product is lost or destroyed, neither your experts nor the company's experts are able to examine the product for defects. It is your burden to prove that the product was defective. So if the product cannot be examined, you may not be able to prove your case.

COST

Products liability cases are very expensive to pursue. Expert engineers must testify concerning the defect in the product. The big corporations involved with the design, manufacture, etc., of the product have cadres of lawyers and big budgets. They hope to "paper to death" the opposition with legal motions, petitions, etc. Your attorney must have the know-how and resources to do battle with the big boys. Many P.I. attorneys refer out the products cases that come to them if products liability is not their specialty. Others take every case that walks in the door, intending to learn each new field as it comes up.

Because of the expense and time involved in the products liability war, the injuries must be serious for the case to be viable. As with medical malpractice cases, unless the case is worth $75,000 or more it will be hard to find a reputable attorney who will take it.

INTENTIONAL INJURIES

Injuries that result from intentional action are resolved quite differently from injuries caused by negligent conduct. Assaults and batteries are the most common kind of intentional injuries. Auto accidents also obviously sometimes result from purposeful conduct. The most important differences between negligence actions and lawsuits arising out of intentional injuries involve the assessment of punitive damages and the collectability of the judgment.

First the good news: Intentional injuries can inflame a jury's passion such that it is moved to award punitive damages against the defendant. These damages are assessed as a means of punishing the defendant for outrageous conduct. Punitive damages can be huge. Recall the verdict of the O.J. Simpson civil jury. Juries sometimes shock everyone involved with the litigation by awarding punitive damages that are way out of proportion to the actual damages suffered. You will read about such verdicts, since newspapers love to report large awards. But under the law, punitive damages must bear a reasonable relationship to the actual damages. What you won't read about is when the court reduces the award because the punitive damages were excessive. That's the bad news.

Now for the really bad news: Jury verdicts for intentional injuries are often uncollectible. Most insurance policies provide exclusions of coverage for intentional injuries. The courts uphold these exclusions since it is considered bad for society for individuals to be able to insure themselves against their intentional acts that injure others. The reasoning is that if you can insure yourself against assaulting others, the threat of a financially ruinous lawsuit will be reduced and you might be tempted to carry out your secret desire to assault the object of your disaffection.

That is rightfully considered contrary to public policy and against the common good. Thus, the insurance company will not have to pay the judgment returned against its insured. That is why lawyers usually do not try to prove that the injury was caused intentionally unless the individual defendant is wealthy.

If there is no insurance coverage, you must try to collect from the individual. This can be difficult, if not impossible, as well as time consuming and expensive. Even if you have the stomach to try to enforce a judgment by compelling the sale of the defendant's assets, you may be surprised to learn that the defendant has divested himself or herself of all such assets or never had any in the first place. Or you may find that the defendant has filed for personal bankruptcy to avoid your collection efforts. This is another example of winning the battle but losing the war. You never declare victory in a personal injury case until the check clears the bank.

Libel and slander cases are also considered intentional injury cases. Although you often read about multi-million-dollar jury verdicts in these cases, large verdicts almost never stand up on appeal. Journalists have the mighty shield of the First Amendment to protect them. The First Amendment makes it practically impossible for anyone but private individuals to collect for libel or slander. Thus, journalists are free to say practically anything they want about public figures (politicians, entertainers, athletes) without worrying about legal liability.

Slander suits between private individuals are not often profitable. Damages are difficult to prove since insults rarely result in actual financial losses. Collecting on a judgment against a private individual is difficult and unpleasant. Practically, about the only defamation case that is worth pursuing would be if a journalist prints a falsehood about a private individual and that defamation causes provable financial harm. For example, if a newspaper falsely printed that an accountant was arrested for drug trafficking, that would be a case worth investigating.

FOOD POISONING CASES

"Food poisoning" cases are difficult to pursue and usually settle for no more than "nuisance value." Many personal injury lawyers refuse to take them. Because the lawyer is compensated only upon settlement, the relatively low value of most of these cases along with the problems of proof make them generally a poor investment of the lawyer's time and money.

The lawyer must make a business judgment here. He or she may take the case if the client has made referrals in the past. No lawyer likes to lose a good client. If the lawyer makes the economic judgment that the case shouldn't be pursued, he or she can still keep the client if he or she is careful. I make clear to clients with weak cases that my reluctance to represent them does not mean that I don't believe that they were hurt. I let the client know that I am not making light of their injury. I tell the client that I simply can't make enough money on the case to justify pursuing it. Most clients understand this kind of reasoning. Hopefully the client will simply drop the case at this point. Unfortunately, many undoubtedly begin "lawyer shopping."

To prove a "food poisoning" case, it is helpful if the food is kept intact for examination by an expert. You should go to a hospital for blood and stool samples. The injuries in this type of case may be strictly psychological.

Of course, if you have been severely harmed by a contaminated food product, you need to immediately find a good personal injury lawyer. For example, a negligently packed canned food product can cause serious bacterial diseases such as botulism. Be sure if you have been so victimized that the food product is kept in a safe place where it will neither be thrown away nor exposed to heat. Depending on the food product, it should probably be stored in the refrigerator or freezer. Your lawyer will instruct you as to the best way to handle this situation.

PSYCHOLOGICAL INJURIES

Psychological injuries can be an important part of a personal injury case. Post-traumatic stress syndrome is a provable phenomenon that adds "value" to some cases. This syndrome may involve headaches, nausea, dizziness, inability to concentrate, depression, irrational fears, etc. But this is also an area that is fraught with danger for you, the claimant.

The claim for a psychological injury opens your psychological history up for inspection. This can create issues which impede a favorable settlement. The insurance company's lawyer may be entitled to subpoena your psychologist's records. If these records disclose, for example, that the psychologist believes you are a liar, the insurance company has found a potent weapon for court. The company may become unwilling to offer a fair settlement now that it has this damaging bullet in its gun.

Judges, juries, and insurance companies often view psychological injury claims with suspicion. Many people feel that these kinds of claims are usually either faked or exaggerated. Others feel that you should simply deal with "hurt feelings," and financial compensation should not be awarded. Finally, the jury might view you as greedy for pursuing a psychological injury claim. It is not advisable for a client to pursue such a claim unless the psychological injury is serious and believable. Where the claim is real and provable, and where damaging information that can come out during discovery is minimal, psychological injury claims can and should be pursued.

The law, in some states, seeks to weed out many of these claims by requiring that a physical manifestation accompany the psychological injury. For example, psychological injuries often occur in car accident cases. You may develop a fear of riding in cars after a serious accident. If there is a physical injury, the psychological injury can be pursued. But if there is no physical injury, in many states other physical manifestations must be present for you to be able to pursue a claim. Thus, at the very least, headaches, nausea, vomiting, etc. must exist to collect for this kind of claim.

WORKERS' COMPENSATION

If you are injured on the job, you may be entitled to workers' compensation. Laws vary from state to state. The discussion that follows tracks the law of Pennsylvania. You should consult an attorney in your area to be sure there are no important differences that apply to your case.

Workers' compensation pays the medical bills and lost wages of individuals injured or killed in the course of their employment. It is not necessary to prove that your employer was at fault for the accident, because workers' compensation is administered under a no-fault system.

The tradeoff for receiving benefits without having to prove negligence is that you cannot sue your employer for compensation for your pain and suffering. Thus, workers' compensation cases differ from ordinary injury cases in two respects: (1) In a non-work related injury you must prove fault to collect, while in workers' compensation you need not prove fault; and (2) You can collect for your pain and suffering in non-work related accidents, but you cannot so collect when you are injured at work.

There are some exceptions to these rules. If your employer does not carry workers' compensation insurance, you can sue your employer for your pain and suffering. If your injury at work was caused by some individual or company other than your employer or a co-worker, you can collect workers' compensation benefits from your employer's insurance and still have a lawsuit for your pain and suffering against the individual or company that caused the accident.

Your attorney's involvement will also differ, depending upon whether your injury occurred during the course of your employment. In non-work related accidents, the personal injury attorney hopes to get involved with the case at the very earliest opportunity so that a prompt investigation of the accident can be completed. In workers' compensation cases, the individual generally can pursue the claim without the services of an attorney. It is only when the claim is denied that is necessary to obtain the services of an attorney.

The workers' compensation attorney generally receives 20% of the benefits paid. In non-work related accidents the personal injury attorney generally charges $33\frac{1}{3}$% of the settlement or verdict.

MEDICAL TREATMENT FOR YOUR INJURIES 5

THE M. D. V. THE CHIROPRACTOR

There has been a debate raging in the medical community about the comparative merit of chiropractic treatment and treatment by a medical doctor. While I do not offer an opinion as to the therapeutic value of each form of treatment, I can interject a legal perspective into this debate.

After an accident I ask the new client if he or she has a family doctor who can treat his or her injuries. I always prefer that the patient choose his or her own doctor rather than making a referral myself. This helps to avoid the impression that the client's medical care was undertaken merely to build a legal case rather than to treat the client's injuries. When the client needs a referral from me, it becomes necessary for me to choose a chiropractor, medical doctor, or an osteopathic physician.

I generally prefer to initially refer clients to a medical doctor. Insurance companies and their lawyers are often very skeptical about the severity of the injuries claimed. Insurance companies tend to view the opinion of a medical physician as more credible than that of a chiropractor or an osteopath. Regardless of who actually provides the better treatment, I initially lean toward the M.D.

Nevertheless, the value of chiropractic and osteopathic care during the course of treatment for some personal injury plaintiffs is clear. There have been countless occasions over the years where the medical care offered by the M.D. proves insufficient. Often the only treatment that significantly relieves the trauma victim's pain is chiropractic manipulation. Thus, if a period of three to six months has elapsed without significant improvement in the client's condition, it is time to consider shifting the focus towards chiropractic or osteopathic care. I cannot tell you how many times such a shift has resulted in an almost immediate improvement in the client's symptoms. Each of the various disciplines has its strengths and weakness, and a flexible approach to this problem is most helpful.

PHYSICAL THERAPY

It is essential that you enter into a physical therapy program as soon as possible after either a motor vehicle or fall down accident. The muscles in the neck and back can go into spasm shortly after an accident in order to protect the area from further injury. Physical therapy helps to relieve the spasm and the accompanying pain.

During whiplash type injuries, ligaments can be damaged. Ligaments are very strong attachments that keep joints in alignment and limit joint movement to a normal range. Tight ligaments are essential to keep the cartilage firmly in place within a joint and to prevent excessive movement of body parts. Physical therapy teaches the muscles to support the skeletal system when the damaged ligaments have become stretched out. Physical therapists use any of a number of techniques to reduce spasm and pain and to rebuild the weakened musculature.

During the initial months of therapy, treatment generally involves moist heat, ice packs, massage, and ultrasound for deep muscle stimulation. As the body responds and the spasm is relieved, the therapy moves toward rebuilding the muscles that have atrophied during the initial therapy.

The therapist supervises an exercise program to help the patient regain pre-accident strength. Upon conclusion of the therapy program, the therapist instructs the patient in exercise techniques that can be undertaken at home or at a gym.

"Good Injuries"

One of the more ironic, and telling, phrases used by some personal injury lawyers is "good injuries." P. I. lawyers love to call each other on the phone or gather over a pitcher of beer to talk about their cases. Two favorite topics are the new cases that have come into the office and cases that need to be evaluated for settlement purposes. In both of these cases the severity of the injuries is high on the list of topics to be discussed.

I kid you not—I have heard P. I. lawyers in all seriousness refer to painful injuries their clients have suffered as "good injuries." For example, I might tell another lawyer about a case in which a six-year-old child ran out into the street after a bouncing ball and into the side of a moving car. If the child suffered a fractured femur which required surgery, the other lawyer might remark, "tough liability, but good injuries." I also recall the time I told a lawyer I worked for that a client needed surgery. I was stunned to hear him reply, "Good."

The "good" of course means a good chance of recovery of damages. An injury of sprains and strains usually isn't as easy to collect on as one that is graphic (like broken bones) and elicits sympathy. In the next chapter I will discuss how the monetary value of an injury is determined.

Keeping Track of Your Treatment

It is very important to make notes regarding your treatment and injuries. Form 10 in the Appendix of this book is a worksheet that should help you with this task. Give your lawyer this worksheet when your treatment concludes. It will help him or her in many ways. It speeds his or her ability to gather all of your medical records. It provides him or her with information to put into the settlement demand letter he or she sends to the insurance company. If it becomes necessary to take depositions, it assists him or her in preparing himself or herself and you for that important part of the lawsuit.

THE SETTLEMENT PROCESS 6

The vast majority of personal injury cases ultimately are resolved through settlement rather than through trial. Therefore we now turn to an examination of the settlement process.

There are various stages at which personal injury cases are most likely to settle. Knowing this will enable you and your attorney to concentrate your settlement efforts around these opportunities. The first chance for settlement occurs shortly after the medical treatment is completed. After gathering your medical bills and reports, your lawyer evaluates your case and then informs the insurance company of the settlement demand. Sometimes that's all it takes to wrap up the litigation.

Often, however, the insurance company makes an inadequate offer of settlement. If the firm refuses to raise their offer to a legitimate level, then a lawsuit has to be filed. Once it is filed, the insurance company realizes that you are serious and that it will have to start paying its attorneys if it wants to continue to defend the case. This presents the second opportunity for settlement negotiations. It is common for the company to make a reasonable settlement offer immediately after your attorney files the lawsuit.

If the case isn't settled at this point, it probably will be several more months before further negotiations take place. Only after your deposition will the next settlement opportunity arise. At the deposition the insurance company's lawyer questions you under oath about the accident and your injuries. This is the first chance for the insurance company to evaluate you in person. How you present yourself at your deposition dramatically affects the settlement negotiations. If you have been properly prepared for the deposition by your attorney, it is very likely that the company will extend an increased settlement offer shortly afterwards.

The final opportunities for settlement occur after a settlement conference and "at the courthouse steps." Judges almost always push hard for settlements at these conferences. The attorneys and their clients may find the judge's arm twisting irresistible and settlement may result. If it doesn't, the judge will order the case to trial. When faced head on with this prospect, one side or the other may finally see the wisdom of settling out of court.

Attempts at settlement by your attorney are often perceived by the insurance attorney as a sign of weakness or desperation. This discourages serious settlement negotiations early in the litigation process. The insurance company may similarly feel that your attorney will see an early settlement offer as a sign of weakness. Relatively large P. I. cases almost never settle without the filing of a lawsuit. If you have been seriously injured in an accident and your lawyer is trying to push a settlement on you even before he or she has filed a lawsuit on your behalf, lights should flash and bells should ring in your head. There's a great chance that you'll do much better with a lawyer who will file the lawsuit and hold out for a better offer.

Experienced plaintiff's lawyers know that in cases involving serious injuries, full value will probably not be offered until after the discovery process has run its course. There is a caveat here though. If the insurance lawyer uncovers damaging evidence during discovery, the settlement value of the case may drop. The lawyer and client need to maintain clear lines of communication to keep unexpected surprises are kept to a minimum.

Your lawyer understands that the most favorable settlements are often reached by waiting out the litigation process. This helps to explain why so many settlements take place only after the parties reach "the courthouse steps." Lawsuits become endurance tests in which each side attempts to wait out the other. It's like a war of attrition.

It's also a lot like the mentality that prevails in the countries in the Middle East. In Israel and the Arab countries, movement toward peace takes place in slow, halting steps. One reason for this is the feeling that one country's step toward peace will be perceived by the other side as a sign of weakness. This leads to lots of strutting threats and little calm dialogue. Intermediaries are needed to grease the wheels of the peace process. Similarly, independent third parties are invaluable in resolving litigation. One aspect of this peace process, known as Alternate Dispute Resolution, is discussed on page 79.

The injured victim and his or her lawyer want a prompt and fair settlement for obvious reasons. Insurance companies also prefer to settle cases without excessive litigation where it is clear that their insured was at fault and real injuries have been suffered. While insurance companies often use delaying tactics in order to hold onto the settlement money as long as possible, they prefer to settle where the only alternative is paying their lawyers large fees to defend meritorious cases. This is why it is absolutely vital that your lawyer demonstrate that it is in the best interest of the insurance company to settle the case quickly and for a fair sum of money.

The best way to convince an insurance company of this is by accurately and completely documenting both the severity of the victim's injuries and the defendant's complete or substantial responsibility. This requires prompt investigation of the accident by your lawyer and his or her investigative team and careful monitoring of the victim's treatment and medical progress. It also requires clear communication between lawyer and doctor so that the opinions in the medical report are stated in a legally acceptable way.

Once the lawyer proves to the insurance company both that it must compensate the victim for his or her injuries, and that those injuries were significant, the company realizes that a jury or arbitration panel is likely to return a large award against it. You will have maximum bargaining power when you, your lawyer, and the insurance company all realize that the company is "on the hook." Rather than pay large sums of money to both you and its lawyers, the company will likely choose to cut its losses at this point and make a settlement offer.

The insurance companies often have a big bargaining advantage over you. The money rests in the company's bank account or investments drawing interest throughout the case. Your lawyer needs to push the firm to release its grip on some of that money. You, on the other hand, may badly need the money to pay your bills and live your life. Or worse, your lawyer may need to settle some cases for his or her own personal reasons. Insurance companies can smell desperation. If the insurance company senses that you or your lawyer is desperate to settle the case, it will make at most a small offer.

Insurance companies use different tactics to increase their bargaining power over you. One such tactic is the delay game. The companies know that extended delays deepen some plaintiffs' desperation. The subpoena game is another annoying tactic. Insurance lawyers engage in extended "fishing expeditions" in which they subpoena documents from every imaginable area of your life, hoping to hassle, embarrass, or find something to use against you. As I write this I have a case going on involving a 36-year-old Harvard University educated architect. The insurance company has subpoenaed everything, even his high school records. I wonder if his grammar school records are next.

The insurance company hopes to find damaging information this way. They also use the subpoena game to intimidate plaintiffs into believing that no area of life is private. In reality, if the subpoena game goes too far, your lawyer can seek a protective order from the court prohibiting overly invasive subpoenas. For example, it is improper for the company to subpoena records from your psychologist where you are not making a claim for a psychological injury. Your lawyer should ask the court to "quash" such a subpoena.

The paper game is another favorite. The insurance company lawyer files essentially meaningless petitions and motions in an attempt to "paper to death" your lawyer. This tactic is especially useful against overworked plaintiff's lawyers. Such a lawyer might be willing to settle for less than full value just to reduce his or her workload.

Your lawyer must not allow the company to know that either you or he or she is desperate to settle the case. Yet the lawyer must also keep up the pressure on the company to encourage it to think about settling. It takes finesse, and more than a little acting ability sometimes, to pull this off. It takes a balance of assertive offensive maneuvering and calm defensive stratagems to achieve the desired effect.

Once the insurance company makes an offer of settlement, the ball moves into your court. If the insurance company's offer is acceptable, you must sign a legal document that sets forth the terms of the settlement. This document is called a "release." Form 22 is a sample release. By signing a release you give up the right to ever bring additional claims against the insurance company, even if your injuries turn out to be more severe than you thought at the time of settlement. At the end of a war, the countries sign an armistice agreement that sets forth the terms of peace. The release is the litigation equivalent.

If the offer is not acceptable, the litigation continues. At this point you and your lawyer should decide just what additional "value" the case has.

PLACING A MONETARY VALUE ON AN INJURY

Some people object to the very concept of compensating injured accident victims with money. They might feel that individuals who have been injured should simply be strong and bear their losses. After all, their no-fault insurance should cover their medical bills and lost wages. It is a good bet that these people have never been seriously injured in an accident. Nor is it likely that anyone in their family has suffered such a fate. Nevertheless, it is fair to debate the issue of directly translating pain into dollars.

Some may feel that it demeans the value of human suffering to place a financial value on it. Yet that is the only method our legal system has to redress the injurious acts committed by negligent motorists, shop owners, corporations, etc. And as long as this method of compensation is available, injured accident victims and their attorneys will seek to receive maximum financial redress for the injury. That is human nature.

Still others point to the added costs of doing business they feel that injury lawsuits cause. They believe that these added costs are passed on to the consumer in the form of higher prices. There is some merit to this argument. I believe it is worth paying these higher prices in exchange for keeping the right to sue for compensation. Not only can financial compensation help to make the accident victim whole, but the threat of lawsuits keeps companies accountable for their errors. Consider also that *The Bible* at Exodus 21:25 authorizes financial compensation for pain inflicted by another.

Pending further changes to our present set of negligence laws, individuals are free to look to the courts for financial compensation for injuries caused by the negligent acts of others. Given that this system, or some form of it, is likely to remain in effect for many years to come, the question becomes: How much is an injury case worth? Unfortunately, there is no way to know for sure what a case might settle for until the medical treatment is concluded and the doctor's prognosis rendered.

Unless he or she has been in many accidents and sued many times, the average client has no idea of the amount for which a personal injury case should settle. The client's fate, for all intents and purposes, is in the hands of the attorney. If the attorney, for whatever reason, wants to settle the case, even though fair value has not been offered, how is the client to know? There are no easy answers here, which is why it is vital to retain a lawyer you can trust. I know of no other area of life, with the possible exceptions of going to your doctor or getting your car repaired, where the unsophisticated client has to trust so fully the honesty and good judgment of another.

Lawyers and insurance adjusters evaluate personal injury cases in many ways. For simple cases, such as neck and back strains and sprains (soft tissue injuries) that heal over time, the key factors will be length of treatment and, perhaps, the amount of the medical bills. Some adjusters and lawyers just multiply the total of the medical bills by three or four to determine the settlement value. That is an overly simplistic approach that is used less these days than in the past. Yet medical bills still figure into the settlement evaluations in this kind of injury case. The bills are also considered to a lesser extent in more serious injury cases.

Perhaps the one rule of thumb for these "soft tissue injury" cases is $2,000 for each month of treatment. Thus, a soft tissue back and neck injury with 3 months of treatment will probably settle for between $5,000 and $7,000. There is a limit to this kind of computation. After perhaps 6 or 7 months of treatment, the insurance company may begin to suspect that the claimant is prolonging the treatment just to drive up the settlement. It is, of course, totally inexcusable to stay in treatment one visit longer than is necessary to recover from your injuries.

Ruptured discs, bone fractures, and injuries resulting in scarring generally are compensated more generously than are soft tissue injuries. Insurance companies more often than not suspect that soft tissue injuries are imagined or exaggerated. Herniated discs, fractures, and scarring cannot be faked, at least not without the assistance of a quack doctor.

The severity of the injury greatly influences the settlement offer. So will the characteristics of the individual. For example, a facial scar on an attractive young woman is "worth" far more than an elbow scar on an elderly man. A permanent injury to a child brings a far larger offer than will a similar injury to an adult. A herniated disc suffered by a skilled manual laborer has a greater "value" than a herniation sustained by a person with a sedentary job. A soft tissue injury sustained by a person with a long history of suing for accidents brings a lower offer than the same injury suffered by a first time plaintiff.

The largest jury awards, and therefore the largest settlements, involve severe head injuries, loss of limbs, paralysis, and death. Even these catastrophic injuries must be carefully documented to achieve maximum settlement value. It is especially important with catastrophic injuries for the insurance company to realize that your lawyer knows how to prove these kinds of cases. Claims adjusters are terrified of the huge jury verdicts returned on cases involving severe, permanent injury.

The other factors that influence settlement value include: 1) the reputation of your attorney, 2) the reputation of your doctor, 3) the amount of property damage, 4) the amount of time missed from work, and 5) the willingness of you and your attorney to hold out for top dollar. These factors are important in all personal injury cases.

The reputation of your lawyer is crucial. If your lawyer is known by the insurance companies and their attorneys as someone who knows how to prove a personal injury case, you will get a much better offer than if your lawyer is unknown or is known to be incompetent or inexperienced. The insurance company wants to settle relatively quickly with the knowledgeable, experienced P. I. lawyer because it fears that this lawyer will obtain an arbitration award or jury verdict far in excess of the usual settlement value.

Your doctor's reputation is important. There are many doctors who are notorious for having a patient base made up almost solely of personal injury plaintiffs. Insurance companies suspect that many of these patients are faking or exaggerating their injuries. Naturally, the insurance company resents this kind of case and will not offer top dollar. The company may wish to investigate the case very closely for fraud. If you find that the office of the doctor your lawyer referred you to is crawling with shady looking characters with soft collars around their necks, or if you notice that the patients are treated as if on an assembly line, you probably ought to seriously consider finding a different doctor—and a different lawyer too.

In auto accident cases the amount of damage to the cars is viewed with interest by the attorneys and the insurance company. A lot of damage suggests that there was a strong impact and the injuries are legitimate and possibly serious. A small amount of damage emboldens the insurance company to make a small offer, if they make any offer at all. The suspicion that you may not really be hurt arises again here. The insurance company may be willing to roll the dice on the hope that the arbitrators or jurors will not believe that you were really hurt. Particularly suspicious are the cases where the damage to the vehicles is minor and you run up huge doctor bills at the office of one of the notorious doctors. Get ready for a long and ugly battle or a very low settlement if your case fits this profile.

If you were forced to miss time from work because of your injuries, this increases the settlement value of your case. Some people can't afford to take time off, even if their doctor believes that they should. That's a decision each individual has to make for himself or herself. I recommend that you take a break if you can afford it. The time off can help you to a speedy recovery, and it will help the value of your case. Insurance companies assume that people who don't miss time from work aren't hurt very badly. For auto accident cases, if your car was insured and you didn't waive wage loss benefits, you should be eligible to recover lost wages from your insurance company. If you have no wage loss coverage, your lost wage claim is added to your settlement demand against the defendant.

The willingness you and your attorney have for holding out for top dollar is another important factor. Insurance companies always start with a relatively low offer and work their way up. Your attorney is ethically required to report each and every offer to you. If your attorney knows what he or she is doing, he or she will tell you if the first offer is too low. He or she will also ask you to be patient. This patience almost never fails. The insurance company inevitably increases the offer if they are convinced that you cannot be bought off cheaply. Generally speaking, the longer you hold out, the higher the offer goes. Every case has its limit, though. If your lawyer knows what he or she is doing, he or she will settle when the offer reaches that limit.

So you are probably asking yourself at this point how the lawyers and insurance adjusters figure that limit. Good question. The personal injury lawyer relies on his or her experience in similar cases and on the opinion of other personal injury attorneys to gauge the maximum settlement value of a case. I constantly consult other P. I. lawyers, both plaintiff's lawyers and insurance company lawyers, to help me set a fair settlement value on cases. Conversely, I receive calls all the time from other lawyers for my opinion on their cases.

Jury research can also be consulted to determine what juries have awarded in similar cases. Jury verdicts set the market rate for settlements. Thus, if the average jury award for torn knee cartilage with two surgeries and a guarded prognosis is $175,000, it is likely that the insurance company ultimately will offer an amount close to this to settle such a case, provided they believe your lawyer is experienced and competent and the rest of the case is solid. The company will begin by offering much less, hoping to buy its way out of the lawsuit as cheaply as possible. If your lawyer realizes the true value of the case, he or she will hold out until the offer reaches or closely approaches $175,000.

In a major injury case the client must rely especially heavily on the lawyer. Clients simply cannot know the true "value" of their case without an honest lawyer working on their behalf. Clients sometimes try to compare their case to a friend's. Clients often wonder why the offer on their case is less than the settlement received by a friend or family member. Each case is different. It does the client no good to compare apples to oranges. Only after many years of experience with exposure to many similar personal injury cases is it possible to accurately assess the amount for which a particular case should settle.

ALTERNATE DISPUTE RESOLUTION

Alternate Dispute Resolution (ADR) is the latest craze in the never ending effort to reduce court backlogs. Jury trials are expensive and painful affairs. ADR is analogous to the peace talks nations often engage in either prior to or during actual combat. ADR is the legal version of peace talks to avoid the warfare of a jury trial.

There are numerous forms that ADR can take. The principal forms are mediation, binding arbitration, and non-binding arbitration. Only the imagination limits the possibilities here. As long as both sides agree, ADR can take place in virtually any setting, utilizing virtually any procedure.

MEDIATION Mediation involves bringing the sides together before a neutral third party. This third party can be a judge, an ex-judge, a practicing attorney, a professional mediator, or any other individual upon whom both sides agree. The mediator helps the parties to find common ground. He or she doesn't make a decision like a judge, he or she helps to get each side to see the merit in the other side's positions. The mediator also points out weaknesses that the parties may not realize exist in their own case. By bringing the parties together in this setting, the mediator hopes to expedite settlement of the case or, at least, bring the sides closer together. The mediator's neutrality is his or her power. His or her neutral perspective may give both sides the first truly independent evaluation of the case. This can greatly influence the way the parties view the case for settlement purposes. Mediation is most appropriate where both sides see the possibility for settlement. Where one or both sides are firmly entrenched in their position, it is unlikely that mediation will be useful.

ARBITRATION Arbitration is a better settlement device where the sides are entrenched. Binding arbitration may involve a mini or summary trial. The rules of evidence may be relaxed to permit admission of evidence without the formalities required in jury trials. For example, medical reports may be used to prove damages rather than actual medical testimony. This greatly reduces the time and expense of litigation. If the arbitration is binding, the ruling of the arbitrator ends the dispute. If it's non-binding, the ruling is advisory only. Both sides will learn a great deal about the case and its merit during the course of the arbitration. Often settlement takes place shortly after a non-binding arbitration.

HIGH-LOW ARBITRATION

High-low arbitrations are a special kind of arbitration in which each side submits a monetary figure. The arbitrator selects either the high figure, which, of course, is the one submitted by you, or the low figure submitted by the insurance company. He or she will not split the difference.

The reason for this is that it makes both sides submit their absolute best offer, because if they are too far off the arbitrator will choose the other side's figure. If the arbitrator could split the difference, then each side would exaggerate their position. It is kind of like when a parent lets one child break the candy bar in half and lets the other have first pick. Both take great care and precision to achieve the best result.

There are various kinds of high-low arbitrations. This is just one kind. Again, imagination is the key to finding a process on which both sides can agree.

THE LAWSUIT PROCESS 7

THE LAWSUIT DEADLINE—STATUTES OF LIMITATIONS

A sad moment for lawyer and client occurs when it becomes clear that a Statute of Limitations deadline has passed. Statute of Limitations deadlines are legal time limits that control when lawsuits must be filed. If the lawsuit is not filed before the Statute of Limitations deadline, it will be subject to dismissal by the court. It is, therefore, extremely important that you find out the deadline for your case and keep it in mind when negotiating.

Statutes of Limitation vary from state to state, and occasionally they are changed by legislatures. On the following pages is a list of the deadlines for negligence cases as of the time this book was written, along with the statute citations. To be sure of your deadline you should check the law for your state, or ask a personal injury attorney.

Alabama	Code of Alabama §6-2-38	2 years
Alaska	Alaska Statutes §09.10.070	2 years
Arizona	Arizona Revised Statutes §12-542	2 years
Arkansas	Arkansas Stat. Annotated §16-56-115	5 years
California	Civil Civ. Procedure Code §340	1 year
Colorado	Colorado Revised Statutes §13-80-102	2 years
Connecticut	Connecticut General Statutes §52-584	2 years
Delaware	Delaware Code Annotated. §§8107, 8119	2 years
D. C.	District of Columbia Code §12-301	3 years
Florida	Florida Statutes §95.11	4 years
Georgia	Georgia Code Ann. §3-1004	2 years
Hawaii	Hawaii Revised Statutes §657-7	2 years
Idaho	Idaho Code §5-219	2 years
Illinois	Illinois Statutes Ann. §13-202	2 years
Indiana	Indiana Code Ann. §34-1-2-2	2 years
Iowa	Iowa Code Annotated §614.1	2 years
Kansas	Kansas Statutes Annotated §60.513	2 years
Kentucky	Kentucky Revised Statutes Ann. §413.140	1 year
Louisiana	Louisiana Civil Code Ann. art. 3492	1 year
Maine	Maine Revised Statutes Ann. §752	6 years
Maryland	Maryland Ann. Code §5-101	3 years
Massachusetts	Massachusetts General Laws Ann. Ch. 260, §2A4	3 years
Michigan	Michigan Compiled Laws §600.5805S	3 years
Minnesota	Minnesota Statutes Annotated §541.07	2 years
Mississippi	Mississippi Code Annotated §15-1-49	3 years
Missouri	Missouri Statute Annotated, 35 §516.120	5 years
Montana	Montana Code Annotated §27-2-204, 27-2-207	3 years
Nebraska	Revised Statutes of Nebraska §25-208	4 years
Nevada	Nevada Revised Statutes Annotated §11.190	2 years
New Hampshire	New Hampshire Revised Statutes Ann. §508:4	3 years
New Jersey	New Jersey Statutes Annotated §2A:14-2	2 years
New Mexico	New Mexico Statutes Ann. §37-1-8	3 years
New York	N.Y. CIV. PRAC. R. §214	3 years
North Carolina	General Statutes of North Carolina §1-52	3 years
North Dakota	North Dakota Century Code §28-01-16	6 years
Ohio	Ohio Rev. Code Ann. §2305.10	2 years
Oklahoma	Oklahoma Statutes Annotated Title 12 §95	2 years
Oregon	Oregon Revised Statutes§12.110	2 years
Pennsylvania	42 PA Con. Stat. Annotated §5524	2 years
Rhode Island	General Laws of Rhode Island §9-1-14	3 years
South Carolina	South Carolina Code Ann. §15-3-530	3 years
South Dakota	South Dakota Comp. Laws Ann. §15-12-2, 15-2-14	3 years
Tennessee	Tennessee Code Annotated §28-3-104	1 year
Texas	Texas Civ. Prac. & Rem. Code Ann. 2 §16.003	2 years

Utah	Utah Code Annotated §78-12-25	4 years
Vermont	Vermont Statutes Ann. Title 12, §512	3 years
Virginia	Virginia Code §8.01-243	2 years
Washington	Revised Code of Washington Ann. §4.16.020	3 years
West Virginia	West Virginia Code §55-2-12	2 years
Wisconsin	Wisconsin Statutes Annotated §893.54	3 years
Wyoming	Wyoming Statutes Annotated §1-3-105	4 years

You should consult an attorney in your state if you fear that the Statute of Limitations has passed in your case. There are some exceptions you may need to be aware of. For example, generally, minors have two years from the date they reach their 18th birthday to file, although, again, this varies from state to state.

For obvious injuries, like those resulting from car accidents, the time period begins when the injury occurs. However, different deadlines apply to certain kinds of cases. For example, in medical malpractice cases, in most states the time begins on the date you first discovered or should have discovered the malpractice. It is a good idea to start the suit within two years from the alleged malpractice since this may be the date on which you should have discovered it.

One of the worst types of calls a P.I. attorney can get is when a potential client calls and says he or she was badly injured and the Statute of Limitations runs out next week, or tomorrow! A busy attorney will often decline to take such a case because he or she does not want to take the risk that the suit cannot be filed on time, or that he or she will have to file a suit before knowing if there are actual grounds for filing.

Learn your deadline as soon as you can and mark it on all of your calendars. If you delay hiring an attorney, be sure to contact one at least a month before the deadline.

ATTORNEY ERRORS

Occasionally an attorney will simply miss a deadline. This is an embarrassment and a financial disaster for the attorney. Some try to cover up their error by telling the client that their case wasn't as good as they had thought. Others put up some of their own money and tell the client that it was the only settlement they could get. Still others stall for time by telling their client that suit was filed and that the litigation is progressing.

If you believe your attorney has missed your Statute of Limitation deadline through his or her own fault then you should contact a legal malpractice lawyer or the state bar association disciplinary committee.

CHOICE OF TRIALS

The first major choice that must be made regarding the filing of a personal injury lawsuit involves the type of trial you wish to have. You and your lawyer must determine whether to demand a jury trial, a trial before a judge without a jury, or a hearing of a more informal nature. The choice you make may determine how quickly your case is decided and the maximum amount of money you can receive to compensate you for your injuries.

If you and your lawyer select an informal hearing, many states provide an arbitration procedure as the forum for the resolution of your dispute. To illustrate, in Philadelphia Common Pleas Court arbitrations, your case is judged by a panel of three attorneys. These lawyers are chosen at random from a list of all qualified lawyers who practice in Philadelphia County. The Arbitration Center tries to assure that the arbitration panel has one plaintiff's lawyer, one insurance defense lawyer, and one lawyer who does neither plaintiff's nor defense work.

The average Philadelphia personal injury arbitration takes no more than two hours to complete. The lawyers submit medical reports to prove the extent of the injuries. The rules of evidence are greatly relaxed so that the case can be tried quickly and efficiently. The arbitrators reach their decision immediately upon the conclusion of the hearing. This decision is communicated to the lawyers within four days in most cases. Jury trials, on the other hand, can take weeks or longer. Doctors and other expert witnesses must actually testify, and strict adherence to the rules for admission of evidence is required. Trials before judges, also known as "bench trials," take much less time than jury trials but considerably more than arbitrations.

The amount of money damages you can obtain in an arbitration hearing may be limited to a certain dollar amount. This will vary from state to state and county to county. Trials before juries or judges without juries have no such limitations. If you have suffered a serious injury due to someone else's negligence and there is adequate insurance coverage, you will want either a jury trial or a trial before a judge.

These types of trials are considerably more expensive than arbitration hearings. You will probably also have a longer wait before your case comes to trial if you choose a jury trial over an arbitration. Again, in arbitrations, you may be able to prove your pain and suffering through your testimony and your medical reports alone. The added expense in jury and judge trials comes from the expert witness fees charged by doctors and other expert witnesses. This, as you might imagine, can cost several thousand dollars. Thus, if your case is on the borderline, that is, if the arbitration limit is $50,000, and you think the case is worth somewhere between $40,000 and $50,000, you will undoubtedly elect to have your case filed as an arbitration.

If the case is clearly worth more than $50,000, it is probably worth the wait and the additional expense involved with a jury trial. Your lawyer may be able to work out an arrangement with your doctor so that you do not have to pay the doctor's fee for his or her testimony until your case settles.

CHOICE OF VENUE

Often there is a choice of counties in which the lawsuit may be brought. This is known as "choice of venue." For example, if the accident happened in one county, but the defendant resides in another county, your case probably can be filed in either county. In some areas one county has an advantage over other counties because the awards are generally higher. For example, awards are generally higher in inner-city counties than in suburban counties. Thus, even though you may wait longer for trial in a large city, the higher money awards make it worth the wait.

When the accident involves federal law, there may be an additional choice, namely, federal court. For instance, if you are in an accident with a U.S. Mail truck or if you fall and are injured on federal property, the suit must be brought in federal court. Cases based upon civil rights violations, such as police brutality, may also be pursued in federal court. On average, cases decided in federal court result in lower money awards than those brought in state court in large metropolitan areas.

Money awards are highest in big cities because of the characteristics of its residents. In general, the more urban the setting, the higher the average verdict returned by jurors. It seems that big city dwellers are more liberal and more comfortable with socking it to insurance companies than people who live in rural areas. Also, salaries and costs of living are higher in big cities. This apparently makes it easier for big city residents to fully grasp and come to terms with the compensation owed to the injured plaintiff. Perhaps you have your own theory to explain this phenomenon.

POST-FILING BATTLES

Now that the lawsuit has been filed, what happens next? Sometimes the insurance company immediately makes a settlement offer. The lawsuit papers may be just the thing to get the insurance company's attention. Often the case hasn't settled simply because the insurance company just hasn't gotten around to evaluating the case. Once it is served with the suit papers, it will be squarely faced with a choice. If it chooses to contest the case, it will have to pay its attorneys to defend it. Rather than pay its lawyers and then the claimant at the end of the case, the company may begin to seriously consider "buying its peace," that is, making a fair offer of settlement.

If the insurance company does not yet want to settle the case, it will send the suit papers to its attorneys so that a response to the lawsuit can be filed with the court. Lawyers sometimes refer to the initial suit papers as the "Complaint." The insurance company's lawyer may file an "Answer" to the Complaint, or it may file some form of legal objection to the Complaint. Objections are filed when the company feels that the Complaint is in some way technically incorrect.

Once the preliminary objections are resolved, the defendant files an Answer to the Complaint. An Answer is a legal document that admits or denies the allegations contained in the Complaint. The Answer rarely sheds any light on the conflict because it generally contains nothing but denials. The Answer typically denies everything except that which cannot possibly be disputed (such as the names and addresses of the parties). Once these preliminaries are out of the way, the attorneys begin the discovery process. That is where the essence of the conflict begins to emerge.

THE DISCOVERY PROCESS 8

ENDING THE SNEAK ATTACK

In the bad old days, trials were even more like war than they are now. Modern discovery rules have put an end to the sneak attacks that characterized litigation until recently. These days, each side is required to respond to the other side's requests for information concerning the case. If it fails to do so voluntarily, the court, upon the motion of the requesting party, will order the recalcitrant party to provide discovery. If the attorneys do their jobs properly, 90% of what happens at the trial can be anticipated and planned. During the course of human conflict there will always be the element of surprise, and thus, the 10% element of unpredictability in the trial of a personal injury case.

The discovery process involves three stages: 1) interrogatories and exchange of documents, 2) depositions, and 3) the "independent" medical examination.

INTERROGATORIES AND THE REQUEST FOR PRODUCTION OF DOCUMENTS

The first stage of discovery consists of answering written questions (called "interrogatories"), and the exchange of relevant documents. Each side submits a written request for all relevant documents, as well as for answers to these interrogatories. The rules of civil procedure require a response to these requests for information within a short period of time, typically 30 days, although this varies from state to state. If the responses are late or inadequate, the attorney who submitted the requests can file a motion with the court requesting that the court order the other side to provide the documents and adequate answers. Form 18 is a sample Motion to Compel Discovery. Form 19 is a sample of the order the judge would sign.

The documents that are exchanged during this stage of the proceedings include the police report, ambulance report, all medical records, witness statements, property damage appraisals, photographs of the cars, photographs of the scene of a slip and fall, diagrams of the accident scene, insurance policies, etc. The questions involve similar topics. Form 16 and Form 17 are sample sets of interrogatories. The defense attorney typically sends a similar set to the claimant's attorney for his or her client to answer. Unfortunately, these written questions generally do not yield much useful information. Lawyers typically answer them in a vague manner which casts little light on the dispute.

Attorneys tend to provide vague answers to avoid having these answers used against their clients later in the litigation. For example, an interrogatory may ask how fast the defendant was traveling when he or she first saw your car. The defendant may tell his or her attorney that he or she was going 35 m.p.h. at that time. The defense attorney may, however, choose to be less specific when answering this interrogatory. He or she may indicate in the answer that the defendant was traveling "within the speed limit at the time he first saw the plaintiff's car." If, at the defendant's deposition, the defendant testifies that he or she was going 25 m.p.h. at that time, an inconsistency has been avoided.

Form 14 is a sample Request for Production of Documents. The exchange of documents is very useful, since witness statements, photographs, diagrams of the accident scene, property damage appraisals, medical records, etc., all affect the settlement value of the case.

Once this stage of discovery is completed, it is time to begin preparing for stage two of the discovery process: depositions. It is here that the lawyers get the clearest idea yet of the strengths and weaknesses of their case and of their opponent's case.

DEPOSITIONS

The discovery deposition is one of the most important stages in the litigation of a personal injury lawsuit. It is during the discovery deposition that the insurance company's lawyer gets the opportunity to question the accident victim in person about the accident and the injuries suffered. Similarly, at the defendant's deposition, your lawyer is able to discover much about the insurance company's version of the accident. See Form 11 for a sample list of deposition questions. Success on deposition day vastly improves the chance of a prompt and fair settlement.

The discovery deposition gives the attorney the chance to pick the mind of the individual who is being deposed. Depositions are usually held in the office of one of the lawyers. The testimony is taken under oath and is recorded by a stenographer. Thus, extreme care must be taken to accurately describe the accident and resulting injuries. By confronting an individual at trial with clearly erroneous deposition testimony, an attorney can devastate that individual's credibility in the eyes of the judge, jury or arbitration panel. That is why thorough preparation prior to deposition day is a necessity.

Perhaps the most important advice your lawyer can give you during preparation for the deposition is to tell the truth. Even the craftiest lawyer has trouble tripping up an individual who speaks the truth and sticks to it. Clients sometimes think they can outsmart the other lawyer by bending the truth in their favor. More often than not, the other lawyer can figure out when this is happening and can expose the lie. An otherwise meritorious case can be lost by a small lie. Juries, judges, and arbitration panels have no sympathy for liars, even injured ones.

It is also vital not to guess during a deposition. Frequently the other lawyer asks questions to which the witness simply does not have the answer. It is important to remember that a deposition is not a multiple choice test. You do not score points by occasionally guessing correctly. Stick to the facts and testify only to that which you personally know.

Every trial lawyer has seen his or her client's case reduced in value by an incorrect guess. "I don't know" is a fair answer if it is true. The time spent preparing for the deposition will ensure that the witness does not have to rely on this answer too often. "I don't remember" is also fair if you truly don't remember. Sometimes depositions are taken years after the accident. It can be nearly impossible to recall the minute details attorneys routinely seek during a deposition. Again, preparation will minimize the need to rely on this answer. It's far better to admit that you don't know the answer to a question, or that you don't recall the answer, than to venture a guess.

Another key to a successful deposition is to know when to stop answering. Often the defense lawyer uses the deposition as a "fishing expedition" in which he or she hopes to hook absolutely anything of use to the defense case. That is why many questions that seem completely irrelevant to the accident are asked. Believe it or not, this is generally permitted by the courts.

Since the other lawyer is attempting to pick your mind, you must not make his or her job easier by responding to each question with a long, drawn out answer. If a question can fairly be answered with a "yes" or a "no," by all means do that and say no more until the next question is asked. Your lawyer may even tap you on the shoulder or use a pre-arranged signal if your answers are getting too detailed. This signal lets you know to keep your answers brief. If you give the other lawyer enough ammunition, you increase the likelihood that eventually he or she will find something to use against you. That is why brief answers are usually best.

It is vital that you completely understand each question before attempting to give an answer. It is not possible to give a truthful and accurate answer to a misunderstood question. The defense attorney will repeat or rephrase the question if requested to do so.

It is important to speak loud enough so that all in the deposition room can hear the testimony. You should keep your hands away from your mouth. To some attorneys a hand in front of the mouth implies that you have something to hide. Questions cannot be answered with a nod of the head or an "uh huh" or an "uh uh." You must say "yes" or "no" so that the stenographer can record the response.

You should not exaggerate your injuries or losses, but you should not hesitate to explain fully all of the injuries and damages caused by the accident. Watch out especially for questions such as, "Did you suffer any other injuries?" A negative answer at the deposition can limit you at the time of trial. You must think long and hard before committing yourself to such an answer. If you cannot think of any other injuries or complaints, it is fair to tell the other attorney, "That's all I can think of right now." This keeps your options open in case you've simply forgotten about an important part of your claim. It's easy to forget during the pressure of a deposition, especially if the other attorney is utilizing a combative style of questioning.

You should not try to memorize the accident, injuries, and treatment. Justice requires only that you tell your story to the best of your ability. A memorized recitation of the events appears contrived and manufactured. Some degree of spontaneity adds settlement value to the case.

Since you are trying to make a favorable impression on the defense attorney, it is important to dress neatly and to treat all persons in the deposition room with courtesy and respect. There is nothing to gain by arguing with or insulting the defense attorney. After the deposition this attorney will report his or her impressions of you to the insurance company. If this attorney thinks that your attitude will rub the jurors the wrong way, the insurance company will be inclined to make a relatively low settlement offer.

The most import aspect of the discovery deposition is you and the appearance you make. If you give the appearance of fairness, honesty, and earnestness, and if you keep in mind these suggestions, you will have taken a great stride toward the successful settlement of the litigation.

THE "INDEPENDENT" MEDICAL EXAMINATION

The insurance company has the right in every personal injury case to have you examined by a doctor it chooses. This examination represents the third stage of the discovery process. The insurance lawyers like to refer to this as an "independent medical exam" or an IME. The IME is anything but independent and no insurance lawyer will claim otherwise outside the courtroom, that is, not with a straight face. The doctors paid by the insurance company strain to offer opinions that help the insurance company. Also, the IME doctor's medical skills may be secondary in importance to his or her skills at testifying in a compelling and convincing manner.

It is not hard to believe, nor is it hard to understand, why insurance companies primarily employ doctors who are biased in their favor and more proficient at testifying than at treating or diagnosing injuries. They would get swamped in large jury awards if they didn't approach personal injury litigation in this way. Unfortunately, this approach by the defense encourages most plaintiff's lawyers to seek out doctors who are experienced in plaintiff's P. I. litigation. Thus, your doctor also may be chosen for his or her bias in favor of plaintiffs and his or her skill at testifying.

The IME doctor typically will be a friendly, professorial individual who speaks well in public. Trial lawyers know that juries can be more influenced by a doctor whose manner is likable than by a doctor whose medical credentials are superior.

Insurance companies employ "professional expert witnesses," that is, doctors who earn a major portion of their living on the witness stand. These doctors are particularly motivated to make findings that comport with the expectations and needs of the insurance companies that pay their salaries. Your lawyer brings out this bias during cross examination of the doctor. Nevertheless, a skilled IME doctor can wreak havoc on a P. I. case. If the jury likes and trusts this doctor, it will be inclined to believe that you were not hurt as badly as you and your doctors claim.

Smart P.I. lawyers take certain steps to assure that the client is treated fairly by the IME doctor. The lawyer or someone from his or her office should accompany the client to the exam to monitor it. In a particularly complex case, the lawyer may retain a registered nurse to take notes during the exam and to assure that the client is protected. A lawyer should also make clear to the client what to expect during this examination. Form 15 is a sample letter to a client when the defendant schedules an IME.

There is a huge amount of discretion that doctors have in making their findings. Two doctors examining the same patient at the same time may offer dramatically different opinions, depending upon who retained them for the exam. This may be shocking to you but it's the truth. Any personal injury attorney and any insurance company attorney will admit this to you. It's just the way the personal injury war is fought.

The battle of the medical experts is a particularly apt example of the war that is personal injury litigation. Both sides use all of the weapons at their disposal in order to achieve a successful outcome. Without strong weaponry and an effective combat strategy, the battle may be lost. A compelling medical expert witness is a key part of an effective trial strategy.

THE TRIAL 9

PREPARATION FOR TRIAL

If the personal injury case doesn't settle shortly after conclusion of the depositions (see Chapter 8), it is time to begin preparing for trial. It is necessary for the lawyer and client to meet in advance of trial to prepare. There is nothing wrong with a lawyer and client meeting to run through possible questions and answers.

Every lawyer prepares his or her witnesses. Good lawyers prepare exhaustively in hopes of accurately forecasting the questions opposing counsel will utilize. If your lawyer is unwilling to spend the necessary time preparing you to testify, you may want to think about looking for a new lawyer. Witnesses testify much more compellingly when they are confident that the other lawyer will be unable to surprise them with unexpected questions. Preparation helps to assure this confidence.

The preparation session helps to refresh the client's memory and suggests additional areas of inquiry the lawyer may not have thought of already. It also allows the lawyer to see the areas to avoid. One danger inherent in the comprehensive preparation session is that the client will "leave his game in the locker room." In other words, some of the best, most compelling, and heart-wrenching testimony can occur during preparation. Once the emotions have been spent in the lawyer's office, there may be nothing left for the jury to hear. The jury is left with an incomplete picture of the pain, suffering, and emotion bound up in the client's injuries. The plaintiff's attorney will typically try to move the questioning to less emotional areas when it appears the client is achieving catharsis or release in the office, rather than in the courtroom.

Some clients think it is unnecessary to prepare for trial. Many clients resist taking the time to prepare and insist that everything will work out if they simply tell the truth. While having the truth on your side is critical, it is not enough to ensure fair compensation at trial. Careful preparation helps you (or any other witness) to relax so that you can offer testimony in an organized, thoughtful, and convincing way. This helps the jury to understand your testimony, to relate to it and to you in a positive way, to recall it accurately during deliberations, and most importantly, to be motivated to return a large award that fully compensates you.

The substance of your preparation session with the lawyer is privileged information. The defense lawyer is not permitted to inquire about it during cross examination. In fact, all communications between lawyer and client are privileged and private, unless the client waives that privilege.

In the O. J. Simpson criminal trial, the attorneys repeatedly asked on cross-examination about the preparation time spent between attorney and witness. That was permitted because the only real client in the case was O. J. Simpson himself. The detectives and the other prosecution witnesses were not the prosecution's clients. Thus, no attorney/client privilege existed to bar inquiry into conversations between the prosecutors and their witnesses. Similarly, conversations between the defense team and their witnesses, other than O. J., were fair game for cross examination by the prosecution.

Voir Dire—Selecting the Jury

An important stage in the course of a jury trial takes place at the very outset of the proceedings, namely, the "voir dire" (generally pronounced "vwa dear") of the jury. Voir dire consists of questions the attorneys of the potential jurors in order to determine which of those potential jurors will actually sit on the jury panel. Form 20 is a sample set of voir dire questions. Sometimes the judge insists on asking the questions himself or herself with input from the attorneys. Voir dire procedure varies from judge to judge.

You have a very important role to play during voir dire. You can provide your lawyer with your reaction to the various potential jurors. If your gut tells you that a certain individual would be unsympathetic to you and your case, you need to let your lawyer know that. Even a sideways glance by a potential juror can tip you off to some unstated hostility he or she may have for you. Your lawyer will greatly appreciate this information.

You should conduct yourself during voir dire, and throughout the trial, in a respectful and appropriate manner. The jury will begin appraising you and your credibility from the moment it first files into the courtroom at the beginning of voir dire. If your jury feels that you are judging them, they may feel offended. You should therefore strain to avoid this appearance. You should express your feelings about the jury to your attorney in as private a way as possible. Be sure to have a pen and note pad handy to make notes during voir dire. You can use these notes to help you later recall your reactions to the various jurors. You can also scribble off messages to your lawyer during voir dire to advise him or her of your opinion concerning individual jurors.

The first set of questions your lawyer will ask may involve whether any of the potential jurors know you or the defendant, any of the witnesses in the case, the attorneys, or the judge; or if any of the jurors have heard anything about the case. This kind of knowledge probably excludes an individual from sitting on the jury, since they may have preconceived notions about the case. It is considered undesirable in our jury system for jurors to have such notions. We lawyers like to think of jurors as blank slates upon which we attempt to imprint our version of the conflict. Of course, jurors are much more than blank slates. Finding out what's already on those slates is what voir dire is all about.

The attorneys inquire during voir dire into the background and attitudes of each potential juror. These questions are not intended to invade the individual's privacy, although sometimes it may seem that way. The questions are asked so that the attorneys can attempt to assess how the individual will view the case. Your attorney wants people on the jury who are sympathetic to accident victims. The insurance company's lawyer wants just the opposite.

For example, your lawyer may ask if there is anyone who has been sued for personal injuries, and, if so, if that experience created feelings of resentment against people who file personal injury lawsuits. Your lawyer will remove anyone who feels that way from the panel. He or she may also ask if anyone on the panel works for an insurance company. This question serves a double purpose. First, people employed by insurance companies tend not to be especially sympathetic to accident victims. Second, your lawyer may simply be trying to communicate to the potential members of the jury that the defendant is insured. Juries tend to award more money if they feel that an insurance company will have to pay the award rather than an individual.

It is actually highly questionable whether this technique is proper, since the jury is not supposed to know of the existence of insurance. Nevertheless, many plaintiff's lawyers employ this technique as a way of influencing the jury. Similarly, the insurance company's lawyer phrases questions to the jury panel in such a way as to suggest that accident victims should not receive much in the way of compensation. Voir dire thus is important not just because it determines who sits on the jury, but also because it presents the attorneys with their first opportunity to influence the jurors. And woe to the client whose lawyer doesn't take full advantage of this key opportunity.

Many other questions are asked during voir dire. This process may seem quite dull to the average juror. The lawyers, however, are extremely interested in the responses, since the make up of the jury has a momentous effect on the handling of the case. Experienced trial lawyers give this process extremely close attention. In large cases, professionals who specialize in jury analysis may be brought in to prepare a profile of the ideal juror for that case. This helps the lawyer to select favorable jurors and to eliminate those who don't fit that profile. O. J.'s criminal defense lawyers employed consultants for this purpose, and with great success.

Yet many lawyers will tell you that after studying all of the jury research into the type of juror who will favor his or her client's cause, the lawyer picks the jurors his or her gut says should be on the jury. If the jury gives the lawyer a friendly, accepting look or a favorable nod of the head during voir dire, that lawyer will probably want this juror, even if jury research indicates that he or she will be an unfavorable juror.

The attorneys seek a promise from the jurors during voir dire that they will be fair. The lawyers repeatedly speak of wanting nothing more than a fair jury. This is happy-sounding nonsense meant only to convince the jury that the lawyer is a reasonable person. The reality is that each lawyer wants jurors who are sympathetic to their client's cause and unsympathetic to the other side. A jury that is unfairly prejudiced against the other side is ideal.

Fairness is really not the concern of the trial lawyer; that's the judge's concern. The lawyer's business is serving the client's best interests, while, of course, acting always within the bounds and strictures of the ethical rules for lawyers. The American system of jurisprudence is adversarial in nature, and lawyers are expected to practice in an adversarial manner. Theoretically, truth and justice emerge after a legal battle in which each attorney zealously presents the evidence in the light that is most favorable to that attorney's client. It's a nice theory but hardly scientific in its accuracy.

Each attorney in a one plaintiff/one defendant case is permitted during voir dire to eliminate or strike a set number of jurors from the jury without stating the reason. These are called "peremptory challenges." In cases with multiple defendants, the judge decides the number of strikes available to each attorney. There are many different theories that attorneys study in deciding on which jurors to strike peremptorily.

For example, Jewish people, African Americans, and individuals with ancestry from the Mediterranean countries are generally considered sympathetic to plaintiffs. Germans, English, and people from any of the Scandinavian countries are often preferred by defense attorneys. People who have been sued in the past or who have families employed in the insurance industry or in other exacting professions are thought typically to be unsympathetic to personal injury plaintiffs. Married men and women are preferred by attorneys representing minor plaintiffs. Female jurors are considered by many to be unsympathetic to female litigants, especially young, attractive litigants. The preferred age for a juror from a plaintiff's perspective is someone who is between 30 and 55 years of age.

The attorneys are basically free to strike potential jurors who fit into certain profiles, subject of course, to the limit in the number of peremptory strikes available. The one exception involves race. If a pattern of striking emerges that appears to be based solely on race, this can be challenged legally by the other side. This form of challenge is most frequently made in criminal cases. I have not heard much about it in personal injury cases.

Jurors who appear through their answers to be unfairly prejudiced in some way concerning a matter of importance in the trial can be removed "for cause." There is no limit to the number of jurors who can be struck "for cause." If, for example, a juror admits that he believes that people who have been injured due to the negligence of another person should not be able to sue for their pain and suffering, that juror will be struck from the jury "for cause." Or if a juror admits that she believes insurance companies should always have to pay, regardless of who caused the accident, that juror will be struck "for cause." After all of the strikes have been utilized, the jury will be set and the trial can begin.

The jury in personal injury cases consists of active and alternate members. The alternates hear the case but take part in the deliberations only if an active juror is removed from the jury during the trial for sickness or for some other reason.

OPENING STATEMENTS

Jury trials begin with the attorney's opening statements. Your lawyer addresses the jury first. The defense lawyer can choose to address the jury immediately after your lawyer finishes, or he or she can wait until you have finished presenting all of your evidence. Most defense lawyers open immediately after your lawyer's opening.

Opening statements are an extremely important stage of the proceedings. The attorneys are permitted here to tell the jury what the case is about and what the evidence will show. It is also the second opportunity the attorneys have to influence the jurors. The attorneys seek to build upon the trusting relationship they began cultivating during voir dire. The idea here is to get the jury to identify with the lawyer's client and his or her case.

Jury research indicates that 80% of jurors make up their minds as to liability for the accident after the opening statements and never change those initial beliefs. Accordingly, smart trial lawyers treat this area of the trial with careful preparation and deep respect.

It is absolutely crucial that the opening statement be interesting to the jury. The trial lawyer's worst nightmare is a boring opening address. It is extremely difficult to persuade an inattentive jury. Experience has shown that one of the best ways to get and keep the jury's attention is to turn the opening address into the telling of a story. The skillful trial lawyer attempts to weave a tale concerning the events of the accident and the plaintiff's injuries which gives the jury an interesting context for the case. A boring car accident case can be enlivened by this story-telling technique.

Perhaps the opening address might begin as follows: "April 11, 1997, began as an ordinary day in the life of John Jones. He awoke, made his coffee, talked to his wife and kids, and got ready for work. Little did he know that the events of that day would change his life. Come with me as we journey back to that momentous day in John Jones' life. Come with me as we watch the events unfold that would leave John Jones with the shattered life and dreams he must cope with today." What juror could sleep through that?

Lawyers often choose a theme for the case which they first refer to during the opening statement. This gives the jury an interesting point of reference that hopefully will make the evidence easier to understand and apply during deliberations. The lawyer then returns to this theme during the closing argument in order to create a sense of completeness and closure in the jury's mind.

For example, for a grocery store slip and fall case, your lawyer may use the theme of consumer expectations. He or she will speak of the store's failure to meet those expectations and how the accident resulted from that failure. That's got to be more interesting to the jury than a dry recitation of what the evidence will be. The attorney may also weave interesting and familiar analogies into the opening address. He or she may compare a scarred face to a damaged work of art. He or she may point out the economic value society places on art in the hope that the jury will value an intact human body even more. The trial lawyer will do whatever it takes to get and keep the jury's attention and empathy during the opening statement. You should feel free to suggest to your lawyer appropriate themes, analogies, or stories for your case.

Lawyers make certain promises to the jury in the opening about what the evidence will show. It is a foolish lawyer that makes a promise that he or she cannot keep, since the opposing lawyer will pounce on unkept promises. If the trial has gone as planned, the lawyer reminds the jury during closing argument of the promises made during opening statements and how those promises were kept. This helps to tie the whole process together in the jury's mind and helps it reach clear conclusions about who should prevail and for how much.

Your Part in the Case

DIRECT EXAMINATION

Your case usually begins with your testimony, both on direct and cross examination. Your testimony is perhaps the most important part of the trial. No matter how skillful and prepared the lawyer is, if the jury doesn't like or doesn't believe the plaintiff, the result will not be favorable.

Direct examination involves your testimony in response to your lawyer's questions. The initial questions typically are simple and concern background information, such as education, family, and employment. These simple questions give you a chance to relax on the witness stand in the role of plaintiff. They also provide the jury with information that may help them relate to you. Your lawyer wants the jury to like you so that it will want to compensate you generously for the losses and damages you suffered in the accident

After the initial background questions, the testimony might turn to the facts of the accident. Your lawyer attempts to elicit a favorable and believable recitation of these facts. Hopefully, this will fix a version of the accident in the jury's mind that will stay cemented in place all the way through to the conclusion of the jury's deliberations.

After testifying about the accident, your lawyer may ask you to discuss how you felt physically and emotionally at the accident scene and whether emergency room treatment was required. If the defendant made statements at the scene, this would be an appropriate place for them to come into evidence. Even a simple apology from the defendant at the scene can influence the jury's view of liability for the accident.

The testimony then moves to the days and weeks following the accident. Eventually the jury will hear about the full course of medical treatment and, of course, how you are currently feeling. You may testify about the effect the accident has had on your life and on your family. Employment losses are also examined. Any other relevant aspect of your losses and damages are discussed before the conclusion of direct testimony.

Your lawyer may attempt during direct testimony to take the sting out of unfavorable evidence. If, for example, you have a preexisting medical condition that calls into question the causal relationship between the accident and the injury claim, your lawyer may gently ask you about this medical condition during direct. This gives you the opportunity to discuss the prior condition and perhaps explain the effect the accident had on you. This can defuse an otherwise troublesome aspect of the case. By confronting the problem directly, you avoid the situation where the jury first hears about the damaging information during the insurance defense lawyer's accusatory questioning. This preemptive strike takes some of the wind out of the other lawyer's sails.

CROSS EXAMINATION

To illustrate, during the O. J. Simpson criminal trial, L.A.P.D. Criminalist Dennis Fung and the prosecution case were devastated by the scathing cross examination by Barry Scheck. The jury would have been much less moved by the allegations about Fung's sloppy work if the mistakes had been confronted and disposed of during his direct testimony. He would have been able to calmly explain that although mistakes were made, they were of no relevance to his ultimate findings. The plaintiff's lawyers showed during the civil trial that they had learned this lesson.

After direct testimony concludes, the defense attorney cross examines you. This attorney attempts to discredit you, if possible. He or she may try to show that your version of the accident is unreliable. He or she will also undoubtedly try to prove that your losses and damages are not as bad as you would like the jury to believe. This is where the deposition testimony is so important. If you testified differently at your deposition than at trial, the defense lawyer makes this clear to the jury. If possible, this lawyer also brings out additional deposition testimony that hurts your case. Your lawyer makes similar use of the defendant's deposition when he or she cross examines the defendant.

One of the main purposes of cross examination is to set up the closing argument. Sometimes the lawyer asks questions on cross that seem unimportant to the outcome of the case. The importance may be made clear only during the closing speech. For example, the defense lawyer in a grocery store slip and fall case may bring out during cross examination that your shopping cart was empty at the time of the accident. During closing, the defense lawyer might argue from this that you should have seen the liquid you slipped on, since it was not blocked by any groceries in the cart. Rather than pressing the issue during cross examination to make its relevance clear then and there, saving the issue for closing allows this lawyer to avoid the risk that you will explain away the problem.

This technique is employed frequently during the cross examination of a medical expert. The lawyer doesn't expect to destroy the doctor's credibility. Perry Mason, after all, was only a television show. In real life, the lawyer hopes to make a few points during cross examination and then to attack the doctor's credibility or opinion during closing argument. The technique of a fleet-footed boxer is much safer here than directly confronting the doctor with a series of impeaching questions, especially if the doctor is experienced as a trial witness. The doctor's superior medical knowledge may allow him or her to talk through difficult cross examination. Jab and move, jab and move is the favored practice.

Cross examination style varies from lawyer to lawyer and from cross exam to cross exam. The lawyer should use a style he or she is comfortable with and not try to emulate another attorney's style if it is not a natural part of his personality. Juries can tell when the lawyer is putting on a false personality. I would not try to cross examine a witness using F. Lee Bailey's approach, even though he is one of the best. My cross would come off as forced if I tried to use an inauthentic personality.

The traits of the witness affect the way a lawyer conducts cross examination. The jury may deeply resent the scathing cross of a sympathetic witness. For example, the jury may have great sympathy for an elderly plaintiff who was seriously injured in an accident. Similarly juries view children with sympathy. A jury will punish the lawyer who attempts to torch such a witness during cross. It would be better for the lawyer to make his or her points in a relatively gentle, respectful way and then sit down.

OTHER
WITNESSES

The next witness typically called by your lawyer is an eyewitness to the accident. The same rules and strategies of direct and cross examination apply to this and all other witnesses. The investigating police officer may testify if he or she witnessed key events at the scene of the accident. An accident reconstruction expert may testify if it will help to clarify who caused the accident. This expert relies upon evidence at the scene and witness statements to reconstruct the events leading to the accident. The defense may retain its own expert for this purpose as well. The liability war may turn into a battle of the experts.

Your lawyer may next offer the testimony of members of your family or others familiar with the effect the accident had on you. On cross examination your friends and family members are subject to questions about their relationship to you. These questions seek to show bias of the witness in your favor. Similarly, defense witnesses who are related in some way to your adversary can expect cross examination concerning that relationship.

RE-DIRECT AND
RE-CROSS
EXAMINATION

After the conclusion of cross examination, your lawyer has the chance to ask additional questions on what is called re-direct. Re-direct testimony is supposed to be limited to matters that were discussed during cross examination. The object of re-direct is to rehabilitate you in the eyes of the jury or to answer questions raised by the cross examination. For example, if the defense attorney forces you to admit during cross examination that some part of your deposition testimony was different than your trial testimony, on re-direct you may be able to offer a reasonable explanation for the difference or you may explain why the difference is irrelevant to the accident. The defense lawyer is permitted to conduct re-cross as to any issue raised on re-direct, and so on until all the questions have been asked.

MEDICAL TESTIMONY

Next your lawyer might move to the medical evidence. Your doctors testify about the injuries suffered, the treatment, the diagnosis, the causal relationship between the accident and the injuries, the amount of pain such injuries cause, and the prognosis for the future. If you had to have surgery, that will be examined in great detail. Perhaps plastic models of the affected body part will be used to make the testimony more interesting and understandable to the jury. If future treatment or surgery is required, the doctor offers his or her opinion regarding the nature, duration, and expense of this treatment and surgery.

The defense lawyer on cross examination seeks to discredit the doctor or his or her opinions. For example, if the doctor treats a lot of plaintiffs, the lawyer will imply that this prejudices the doctor and that his or her opinions are slanted. Or the lawyer may confront your doctor with medical journals that support conclusions different than those he or she reached. The cross examination of any witness is limited only by the lawyer's imagination.

It is difficult for a lawyer to completely discredit a doctor in a jury's eyes. Juries often feel that since the doctor was educated in medicine and the lawyer in law, the doctor's view of the injuries must prevail over the lawyer's suggestions. Nevertheless, skillful cross examination of the doctor can cast doubt on his or her testimony. That is generally the most that the defense lawyer can hope for. Similarly, when the insurance company's medical expert testifies, your lawyer is generally satisfied if he or she has cast some doubt on the doctor's opinion. Any chinks in the doctor's armor created during cross examination become grist for the lawyer's mill during closing argument. That is really the most the lawyer can reasonably hope to gain from cross examination of a doctor.

Medical and other expert testimony is often presented to the jury on videotape. Doctors' schedules are so busy, and the course of a personal injury trial so unpredictable, that lawyers would rather have a videotape "in the can" than rely on the doctor's availability for live testimony. The stresses and strains of a jury trial are immense. The additional pressure of balancing a doctor's schedule against a judge's insistence on moving the case forward is something the trial lawyer wishes to avoid. Having videotaped testimony ready for use at the lawyer's convenience greatly relieves this pressure.

Unfortunately, videotaped testimony is much less interesting than live testimony. Trial lawyers die a thousand deaths as they watch the jurors' eyes glaze over during important taped medical testimony. Smart P. I. lawyers keep videotapes short, preferably about 20 minutes in length, since it is difficult for the average juror to continue to closely focus for a longer period of time. The most important points must be made right at the beginning while the lawyer has the jury's attention.

DAMAGES

LOSS OF EARNINGS AND EARNING CAPACITY

Any other significant losses or damages must be proven through the testimony of other expert witnesses or in some other legally acceptable way. For example, if you can no longer perform your job because of your injuries, an economist and a vocational expert may have to testify. This testimony will review the types of work available and appropriate for you and the actual economic losses you will suffer because you can no longer do your job.

Have you ever wondered, after hearing about a multi-million dollar jury verdict in a personal injury case, about the fairness of the jury that returned that verdict? Have you questioned whether any injury could be so severe as to justify such a verdict? The reasoning behind large jury verdicts often can be found in loss of future earning capacity. Compensation for pain and suffering represents only one of several elements a jury must consider when deciding upon a total monetary award in a personal injury case. If the accident victim has suffered lost earning capacity, these economic damages may far exceed compensation for the pain and suffering. Economic damages may include not only lost earnings, but also lost retirement benefits, profit sharing, health care coverage, and other benefits lost due to the inability to work.

You may be able to continue to work, but only at a reduced level of efficiency. This may result in a slower rate of growth in earnings and benefits over the course of your career. These losses can easily be measured and proven at the jury trial through the testimony of an economist. When projected over an entire career, they can become very large. The accident victim who is not employed outside of the home can also expect compensation if that person's ability to render his or her usual household services is reduced by the injury. At present, household services are valued at $12.00 per hour by legally accepted economic studies. These represent real economic losses that can be easily proven at the trial so that fair compensation can be received.

Perhaps an example from a real case will help to illustrate how rapidly these economic losses can add up. A client who suffered a herniated disc in his neck was laid off from his job due to his disability. Even though he immediately found another position, he is claiming losses in excess of $500,000.

The job this client was able to obtain after the lay-off offered fewer responsibilities, smaller wage increases and slower potential for promotions. His retirement and medical benefits were reduced, as were other legally required benefits, such as disability insurance, unemployment compensation, etc. He was also unable to provide his usual services around the household. According to legally accepted research, an employed man in a two-person household spends an average of 7.7 hours per week on household work. At the rate of $12.00 per hour, this loss mounts very rapidly.

The numbers really begin to take off when the reduced earnings and slower potential for promotions are projected over the course of an entire career. While the annual losses suffered by this 35-year-old man are relatively small, the claim becomes quite large indeed, when projected over the next 30 years.

Typically, the defendant retains an economic expert and a vocational expert to rebut this kind of claim. The defendant's economist may question whether the plaintiff actually lost the benefits, salary, ability to perform household services, etc. The defendant's vocational expert will no doubt have quite a different opinion from the plaintiff's vocational expert as to the availability of alternative careers. The bottom line is that both sides present to the jury their view of the plaintiff's economic losses and the jury decides which view is more credible.

Another of my clients had to miss a semester of school because of an injury. While most clients would expect reimbursement from the defendant for any lost tuition, the compensable losses here may go far beyond simple out-of-pocket losses. The lost semester will result in a one-year delay in the start of the client's career. Not only will the client lose a year of earnings and benefits, but that year would have been one of the client's most productive.

We will argue that, were it not for the accident, the plaintiff would have earned a certain salary in 1995. That year would have been year one in his career. Because of the accident, the 1995 salary will actually be earned in 1996, which is the client's new first year. But for the accident, the salary for 1996 presumably would have included a raise over the salary earned in 1995. Year two in a person's career typically includes a raise over year one. This loss will continue every year until the client's retirement. The year that is lost forever is the last year the person would have worked but for the accident. The salary and benefits during that last year are perhaps the most lucrative of the plaintiff's work life. The loss of that year creates a large economic detriment that can be proven through expert economic testimony.

If you have suffered even a seemingly small loss of earnings due to an accident, do not fail to let your attorney know, since the value of your claim can be increased dramatically. Lawyers often overlook this kind of claim because it may appear on first glance to be insignificant. That "insignificant" aspect of your claim can turn out to be its most important part.

LOSS OF CONSORTIUM

Loss of consortium is an additional element of damages in a personal injury claim. Loss of consortium involves damages suffered by your spouse. Your spouse is entitled to be compensated for the reasonable value of the services that you can no longer perform. Your spouse is entitled to remuneration for any loss of support, aid, assistance, companionship, comfort, protection, and love resulting from your injuries.

A good rule of thumb for valuing a loss of consortium claim is to calculate 10% of the value of the case in chief. Thus, if the husband suffered a herniated lumbar disc because of an accident and the case settles for $75,000, it would be reasonable to tack on another $7,500 for the wife's loss of consortium claim.

This kind of claim must be made very carefully. Where the injuries are severe and the loss of consortium legitimate, there is no reason not to pursue a loss of consortium claim. But pursuing this kind of claim can backfire in a big way. If the injuries are relatively small or the testimony concerning loss of consortium not stated in a convincing way, the jury might decide that you and your spouse are greedy for pursuing a loss of consortium claim.

Also, many people prefer not to have this very personal aspect of their life subjected to the searching cross examination of an insurance company attorney. Many people prefer that the most personal aspects of their marital life not be discussed in open court. A loss of consortium claim potentially opens up this kind of inquiry. The defense attorney may be entitled to inquire into the spousal sexual relations that existed before the accident so that this can be compared to the post-accident relations. This is obviously the type of claim which you, your spouse, and your attorney need to discuss in depth before pursuing.

Loss of consortium claims are limited to husbands and wives. Thus, if the injury occurs before the plaintiff's wedding, even if it is just hours before, the spouse is unable to make a loss of consortium claim. Years ago, only husbands were permitted to sue for loss of consortium.

THE BURDEN OF PROOF

Insurance company lawyers love to talk to juries about how the plaintiff has the burden of proof in personal injury cases. This is true but rather meaningless. The burden of proof in civil cases requires you, the injured plaintiff, to prove your case by a "preponderance of the evidence." To win in a personal injury case, your evidence needs merely to outweigh, by any amount, the defendant's evidence. In criminal cases, the burden of proof is "beyond a reasonable doubt," which is a much more onerous burden.

Your lawyer should remind the jury, during both the opening and closing statements, of the easy burden that you must sustain. He or she will also probably ask the jurors during voir dire if anyone has a problem with the concept that the plaintiff needs to prove his or her case by a mere preponderance to prevail. It's a very important point that needs to be hammered home so that the jury decides the case in accordance with the law.

THE DEFENSE CASE

When all the evidence on your behalf has been presented, your attorney rests his or her case. The defense attorney may then ask the judge to dismiss the case for insufficient proof. This virtually never works, yet for technical reasons the insurance company's lawyer often makes this request. Then the presentation of the defense case begins.

The first witness presented by the defense is usually its strongest. Since your evidence has dominated the first half of the trial, the defense seeks to take away your momentum by offering up testimony that is as compelling as possible in favor of the defense. The first defense witness might attack either your version of the accident or the injury claim itself. Perhaps the defendant will testify about how the accident happened from his or her viewpoint. An eyewitness may testify.

If the defense is not contesting fault for the accident, or if it does not have a strong witness on liability, it may put a doctor on the stand to testify about the severity of your injuries.

If the defense lawyer has done his or her job properly, he or she will have carefully prepared his or her witnesses for testimony. This lawyer hopes to persuade the jury to return either a defense verdict or a low monetary award. Carefully prepared testimony will help. Your lawyer gets the opportunity for cross examination after the insurance attorney finishes questioning each defense witness on direct. The roles the lawyers played during the presentation of your part of the case are now reversed. The defense lawyer presents the evidence, and your lawyer then attempts to punch holes in the believability or significance of that evidence.

The defense attorney presents the testimony of all witnesses it has to oppose the plaintiff's case. In addition, the defense offers any other evidence it possesses to support its defense to your claim, such as photographs of the vehicles showing very little property damage. This will work to rebut your claim that the collision caused a serious injury.

In cases involving serious personal injuries, the insurance company frequently engages in surveillance. It may retain an investigator to spy on you. If you are involved in personal injury litigation you need to be on your guard against this kind of tactic. The insurance company may attempt to videotape you engaging in physical activities in order to show the jury that you are not as injured as you claim. Insurance companies have been known to flatten the tires of the plaintiff's car and then videotape him or her changing the tire.

COMPARATIVE
NEGLIGENCE

One of the primary defenses to a personal injury case involves the concept of comparative negligence. To understand this concept, you must first consider that the total amount of negligence involved in the accident equals 100%. This total is divided between the negligence of the defendant or defendants and the plaintiff's comparative negligence. Your recovery is reduced by the comparative negligence.

For example, if the defendant rear-ended your stopped car, the defendant's negligence represents 100% of the total negligence. The verdict is not reduced under this scenario. If, however, the accident involves a defendant who ran a red light, comparative negligence may figure in. If it was determined that you were speeding at the time of the accident and this contributed to the accident, the jury might find that the defendant was 80% negligent and you were 20% comparatively negligent. If the jury determined that the damages justified a verdict of $10,000, the judge would reduce the award by 20% and you would receive $8,000.

ASSUMPTION OF
RISK

A standard defense is the claim that you assumed the risk of injury and, therefore, should not be able to recover damages from the defendant. This is a valid defense to many injury claims. For example, most skiing accidents are not compensable because skiing is an obviously dangerous activity involving frequent injuries. The law in your state may not permit P. I. lawsuits for skiing accidents unless truly reckless conduct can be shown. For example, if the ski resort knew that the design of its slopes was extremely dangerous and failed to warn skiers, it is possible that you would not be found to have assumed the risk of an injury on these slopes.

If you get struck by a batted ball at the ballpark, forget about suing the team, the stadium, or anyone else. When you entered the stadium you assumed the risk that a ball would fly into the stands, possibly injuring you. If you are aware of an obvious danger, purposely elect to abandon a position of relative safety, and place yourself in the zone of danger under circumstances showing a willingness to accept the risk of injury, you cannot collect for your injuries. That's what assumption of risk is all about.

This defense doctrine is often asserted in fall down accident cases. For example, if you are aware of an isolated patch of ice in a parking lot, park your car next to it, and then slip on it; just get up, lick your wounds, and don't even bother to call a lawyer. You assumed the risk of falling when you knowingly parked next to the patch of ice. However, if the entire lot was icy and you had no reasonable alternative route, you can still sue for your injuries.

The assumption of risk defense is generally successful only in the most extreme cases. Don't assume it will bar your lawsuit unless you fit clearly into one of the scenarios I cite here. It is a defense that is often asserted, but rarely prevails.

CAUSATION

It is not enough to show that a defendant engaged in negligent or careless conduct. To recover in a personal injury case, you must prove not just negligence, but also that this negligence was the legal cause of your injuries. Legal cause is shown if the negligence was a substantial factor in producing the harm. An act is not considered a substantial factor in producing the harm if other factors actually caused the harm, and the defendant's act was harmless until acted upon by those other factors. The law in your state may vary in some degree, but essentially that is the way causation works.

I will illustrate with a case which at first would seem clearly to indicate liability on either of two defendants. However, one of the defendants is claiming that his acts were not the legal cause for the accident. My client was driving along the freeway. A tow truck up ahead dropped a tow dolly on the road. The dolly was negligently fastened to the tow truck. My client was able to bring his vehicle to a halt without striking the dolly. Unfortunately, my client's vehicle was then struck in the rear by another vehicle.

The lawyer for the tow truck company is claiming that his client's negligence was not a substantial factor in producing the harm. He claims that, but for the unsafe conduct of the striking motorist, the negligent fastening of the tow dolly was quite harmless. He just might be right since my client was able to stop without hitting the dolly. Even though his client's actions were negligent and even though that negligence led directly to my client's severe injuries, his client may have no legal responsibility whatsoever. His client's actions may not be the legal cause of the accident. The full brunt of the liability may fall upon the striking motorist. Fortunately for my client, the striking motorist was driving a fully insured Federal Express vehicle. There should be no major problem collecting in this case.

OBJECTIONS

Objections are the trial lawyer's tool for preventing the admission of unfair evidence for the jury's consideration. Some of the most frequently made objections are that the question is "leading," "irrelevant," "beyond the scope," "argumentative," "assumes a fact not in evidence," or has been "asked and answered."

LEADING QUESTIONS

A "leading question" is one that improperly leads the witness to the answer sought by the lawyer. For example, "You were driving under the speed limit, weren't you?" is clearly leading. The appropriate wording for such a question is, "How fast were you driving?" Leading questions are permissible when asked of the witness on the other side. Thus, I can properly ask the defendant in a car accident case, "You were driving faster than the speed limit, weren't you?" Similarly, the insurance company's lawyer is permitted to ask that question of my client.

If a witness I present as part of my case surprises me by testifying contrary to my client's interests, I can ask the judge to declare him or her a "hostile witness." If the judge grants this request I can use leading questions. This allows tougher questioning and permits me greater control over the witness. In the O.J. Simpson murder trial, Marcia Clark utilized this technique with Kato Kaelin.

Judges have great discretion in ruling on the "leading question" objection. Many leading questions are asked simply to save time concerning matters that are either relatively unimportant or not in serious dispute. Thus, "Was it sunny on the day of the accident?" is a question that might be permitted by the judge, even though it is clearly leading. In fact, the opposing attorney probably would not object to this question. Attorneys don't assert objections unless they feel there is a good reason to do so. Objections that serve no real purpose, even if they are technically proper, can aggravate the judge and jury, perhaps even creating the impression that the lawyer is trying to hide the truth.

IRRELEVANT "Irrelevant" is a commonly made objection. A question is relevant if the answer sought has any tendency to make the existence of a fact that is of consequence to the determination of the matter more probable or less probable than it would be without the evidence. How's that for legalese? In other words, does the answer really matter to the case?

Sometimes the answer may have some relevance to the case but would be so unfairly prejudicial that the judge will not permit it. For example, if the defendant in a personal injury case had an accident while driving home after an extra-marital tryst, the judge will probably exclude evidence of the affair. While the defendant's pre-accident activities may have some bearing on his state of mind and, therefore, on his operation of the vehicle, this evidence might so prejudice the jury against him that it might blind them to the rest of his testimony. Trials are supposed to be about the events leading directly to the conflict between you and the defendant, not morality plays about private lives.

BEYOND
THE SCOPE

The objection that a question is "beyond the scope" generally occurs in re-direct and re-cross examination. These are the stages of the testimony that take place immediately after the conclusion of direct and cross examination. Re-direct is supposed to be limited to subjects that were explored on cross examination. It is not another opportunity to have the witness restate the testimony elicited on direct. Nor is it a chance to ask questions that slipped the lawyer's mind during direct. If the lawyer attempts to achieve either of these ends, the opposing lawyer should object that the question goes "beyond the scope" of cross examination.

Re-cross is supposed to be limited to the issues raised on re-direct. Re-re-direct should be limited to subjects raised on re-cross. And so on. In this way the inquiry is progressively narrowed until all appropriate questions have been asked. Yet the judge has great discretion here to overrule this objection. Even where the question is clearly "beyond the scope," the judge may permit the question for any number of reasons. Every judge has his or her own practice when it comes to this and every other objection. That's one reason it pays to have a lawyer who tries a lot of cases. Familiarity with the tendencies of judges is a big advantage.

Technically the objection of "beyond the scope" is available during cross examination. Thus, your lawyer may object to an opposing counsel's question on the basis that it is beyond the scope of direct testimony. Realistically, the judge is very unlikely to sustain this kind of objection, since cross examination represents the defense lawyer's first round of questioning. Practically any inquiry that is relevant to the case and is otherwise not objectionable is fair game during cross examination, even if not raised on direct examination. For example, even if I do not question my client about a prior car accident during direct examination, the defense lawyer can certainly ask about this on cross examination. Even though technically this area of inquiry might be beyond the scope, no judge would sustain this objection. It would be foolish for a lawyer to even offer this objection. Again, "beyond the scope" is an objection typically heard during re-direct and re-cross examination.

ARGUMENTATIVE

The objection that a question is "argumentative" is a powerful weapon in the trial lawyer's arsenal. Attorneys tend to get quite carried away during cross examination. This objection reigns in some of the more hotly worded questions. For example, the question, "Do you want this jury to believe that you were only going 25 m.p.h. at the time of the accident?" is argumentative and should be objected to. Questions are supposed to be worded simply, directly, and with the purpose of eliciting useful information concerning the accident. Questions that argue with the witness' statements are objectionable as argumentative.

ASKED AND ANSWERED

The objection that a question has been "asked and answered" seeks to avoid repetition. Attorneys frequently ask a witness during direct examination the same question over and over in order to hammer a favorable point home to the jury. Many judges will sustain the "asked and answered" objection here. This objection is also used during cross examination. If I don't like the answer I got from a defendant the first time I asked it, I may ask it again later in the cross. The astute defense lawyer will object that the question has already been "asked and answered." Judge Ito must have overruled this objection a thousand or more times during the Simpson criminal trial. That's one reason the trial went on for so long.

ASSUMES FACTS NOT IN EVIDENCE

"Assumes a fact not in evidence" is an objection the attorney must keep at the ready. The question, "How fast were you going when you struck the plaintiff's car in the rear?" is inappropriate if it has not first been established that the defendant actually rear-ended you. This is sometimes also referred to as a "foundational" objection. The foundational evidence (a rear-end hit) must first be proved before the question may be asked. The objection here would be either, "I object, Your Honor. The question lacks the proper foundation" or "I object, Your Honor. The question assumes a fact not in evidence."

Objections have other uses as well. Sometimes trial lawyers object to questions that probably are proper simply to send a message to the witness that the question is one of particular importance. The objection will communicate to the witness that he or she needs to take extra care in formulating the answer. The objection gives the witness a couple of extra moments to do just that.

The proper time to make an objection is just as the other lawyer finishes asking the question. If the attorney waits until the question has been answered, the damage may have already been done. The attorney then can only object and "move to strike" the answer. He asks the judge to instruct the jury to disregard the answer. Lawyers typically compare this to trying to "unring the bell." It's an inadequate remedy that the lawyer hopes to avoid relying upon. If the answer was so egregiously improper that it may unfairly influence the jury's deliberations, the lawyer may ask the judge to declare a mistrial. If this request is granted (which rarely happens), the trial ends then and there. The parties then must decide if they want to resume settlement discussions or begin preparing for another trial with a new jury.

CLOSING ARGUMENT

Closing argument represents the lawyers' last chance to directly influence the jury. You will recall that I referred to the lawyers' opening address as a statement. The closing address is more than a statement of the evidence; it is an argument. Whereas the opening statement sets the stage for the trial by informing the jury what the evidence will show, the closing statement goes much further. The lawyers during closing not only sum up the evidence that has been presented, they also argue to the jury about what the evidence means to the case. It is objectionable to make argumentative statements to the jury during the opening address. During closing, they are indispensable.

Each lawyer during closing highlights the most favorable evidence presented during the trial and argues from that evidence certain inferences that are favorable to the lawyer's client. For example, if photographs of the accident vehicles have been presented to the jury and the damage is severe, your lawyer asks the jury to infer from the photos that the collision caused the severe injuries you claim. Further, each lawyer argues that the evidence and inferences mandate that the jury decide the case in favor of their client.

Notwithstanding the O. J. Simpson case, most lawyers hesitate before interrupting their adversary's opening or closing statement. The fear is that the judge, jury, or both, will be offended by the interruption. Many judges feel that it is extremely discourteous for a lawyer to object during opening or closing, and the judge may scold the objecting lawyer in the presence of the jury. This is the lawyer's worst nightmare since jurors generally look to the judge as a respected authority figure. Jurors look to the judge for guidance. If they feel that the judge favors one side or the other, the jurors will, consciously or not, be swayed toward that side.

During closing arguments the lawyers usually remind the jury of the promises made during opening statements about what the evidence would show. The lawyers then suggest to the jury that the evidence indeed showed all that was promised and that the jury, therefore, should return a favorable verdict. The lawyers may also refer to the promises the jurors made during jury selection to be fair and to return a just verdict.

Closing argument generally ends with a brief expression of thanks by the lawyer for the jury's attention and a request for a verdict favorable to that lawyer's client.

JURY INSTRUCTIONS AND DELIBERATIONS

The judge's instructions to the jury represent the very last stage of the trial before the jury retires to decide the case. In his or her instruction the judge advises the jury about the law that applies to the case. The judge uses certain standard instructions but may also permit the lawyers to influence which instructions are given and how they are worded. Form 21 is a sample set of Jury Instructions. I submit proposed instructions like these during personal injury trials. Jury instructions are also sometimes called "points for charge."

If, for example, the accident involves a slip and fall, the judge advises the jury of the degree of care that the defendant was required to exercise for your safety. The judge defines such legal terms as "negligence" and "circumstantial evidence." The judge advises the jury of your burden to prove the case by a "preponderance of the evidence" in order to receive a favorable verdict. The judge may explain that a "preponderance of the evidence" is a far easier burden of proof than "beyond a reasonable doubt," the standard of proof required in criminal cases. "Preponderance of the evidence" requires that your evidence outweigh the defendant's evidence by even the slightest amount. If it does, an award in your favor is appropriate.

The judge advises the jury of the various items of damages it can award. For example, the jury is instructed that, if it believes the defendant is liable to you for the accident, it must award a certain amount of money damages. That amount must fairly and adequately compensate you for the physical, emotional, and financial injuries caused by the accident. The judge advises the jury that past, present, and future pain and suffering should be considered. The judge may also advise the jury to include your medical bills in the award.

If one of the lawyers objects to any part of the jury instructions, the objection must be made before the jury retires to deliberate. That gives the judge the opportunity to correct the instructions, if necessary. If the objection is not made by then, the lawyer waives this objection and may not assert it on appeal. If the objection is made in a timely manner and the judge overrules the objection, the issue is preserved for the appellate court to rule on, if an appeal is filed. If the judge erred in failing to correct the instructions, the appellate court can order a new trial.

THE VERDICT

Now it's the jury's turn to get active. After possibly years of waiting, countless phone calls, letters, doctors' visits, consultations with your lawyer, pre-trial preparation and battles, and the grueling drama of the trial, the jury finally has the case, and your legal fate, in its hands. The answer to the question, "How much?" may be just minutes away.

Sometimes the verdict comes back quickly, and sometimes there are hours or even days to agonize while waiting for the jury to return with the verdict. When it does, the jury foreman announces the decision and the trial is at an end.

THE APPEAL

Just when you thought you were finally free of this legal process, you get the news from your lawyer that there's going to be an appeal. Appeals from jury verdicts are taken for various reasons. Perhaps the judge excluded an important piece of evidence for a reason one of the lawyers felt was improper. If one of the lawyers made inappropriate remarks during his or her opening or closing statement and this was not adequately corrected by the judge, an appeal may be sought. Or possibly, the judge refused to allow one of the lawyers to ask certain questions of the jury during voir dire and the lawyer feels this deprived his or her client of a fair jury. All of these are appealable issues.

A new trial will not be awarded on appeal unless the appealing attorney can prove to the appellate court that something seriously wrong happened at the trial. For example, if you clearly suffered serious injuries, the defendant was obviously at fault for the accident, and yet the jury awarded no damages, the appellate court will order a new trial. If your attorney made a reference in his or her closing argument that was seriously improper, such as mentioning that the defendant had insurance to cover the claim, a new trial will be awarded. The judge will probably sanction (i.e., levy a fine against) the attorney who made this clearly improper remark.

Appeals are often taken for tactical reasons. Even though the party that filed the appeal doesn't truly believe a new trial will be awarded, he or she may file an appeal to try to force the other side to accept a settlement that is less favorable than the jury's verdict. Insurance companies often use this strategy. They figure that if you are desperate for money, you'll take whatever you can get. Meanwhile, the money is sitting in the insurance company's bank account (or more likely tied up in investments) drawing interest. It's a cynical approach, but, after all, litigation is war. The appeal can be a very powerful weapon in the war of attrition that P. I. lawsuits often become.

Understanding "Tort Reform" 10

It is a bad idea to go into an insurance agent's office without having thoroughly thought through the implications of your insurance coverage choices. Insurance agents frequently do not have your best interest at heart, or they may themselves not completely understand how each selection will affect you and your family. If you read and understand this chapter, you will have received some of the most important legal advice I can offer. It's not easy stuff, so take it slow and keep this book handy for fast reference when it's time to choose your insurance coverages. If you have a lawyer, you should call him or her for advice. His or her business success depends in part upon having clients with adequate insurance coverage. If you are a regular client, your lawyer should be happy to help you, free of charge, with your car insurance choices.

Limited Tort v. Full Tort

There are many different types of coverages for car accidents. These coverages vary from state to state. A complete survey of all of the various coverages throughout the country is beyond the scope of this book. The complexity and importance of these choices makes it crucial that you acquaint yourself with the coverages, and the ramifications of the choices you must make, when your insurance policy comes up for renewal. I illustrate this problem by exploring the choices faced by the citizens of Pennsylvania.

Pennsylvania motorists have the option to give up many of the protections that were once included in all insurance policies. For a small savings on their auto insurance premium, they can now choose to give up the right to sue for pain and suffering. This right can be waived for all cases except those involving "serious injury." That is the Limited Tort option. If you are a Pennsylvania motorist and you choose Limited Tort, you remain eligible to sue for your economic losses regardless of the severity of the injury. Thus, you can recover for lost wages, medical bills, and property damage, even if your injury was not "serious." You cannot collect for your non-economic losses, that is, pain and suffering, emotional trauma, etc., unless those injuries were "serious." No one knows exactly what constitutes a "serious injury." This uncertainty can cause the case to be tied up for years of litigation in which the insurance company claims that the plaintiff has not suffered a "serious injury."

The simplest and most important piece of advice I would give to a Pennsylvania motorist concerns the waiver forms used to make insurance choices. By throwing away the waiver forms the agent presents, you avoid the danger of giving up any of your rights. Unless you actually sign and date a form indicating that you choose the Limited Tort option, the Full Tort option will apply to you and the occupants of your car. If you have Full Tort, you retain the unlimited right to sue, regardless of the severity of the injury.

Consider that, if you choose to give up your unlimited right to sue for pain and suffering, you also cause most, if not all, family members living in your household to lose this right. Unless your family member is the named insured on a separate policy with Full Tort, your small savings on your insurance premium forfeits your family's unlimited protection against negligent motorists. Ironically, family members of uninsured motorists retain the right to sue for pain and suffering, regardless of the severity of the injury. Protect yourself and your family by insuring all cars you own and keeping the right to sue for any injuries. Choose Full Tort.

Your state may have a system similar to Pennsylvania's Full Tort/ Limited Tort scheme. Check with a personal injury lawyer before you make such an important choice. Your lawyer should be willing to help you with this, free of charge.

UNINSURED AND UNDERINSURED MOTORIST COVERAGE

I also recommend that you not give up your coverage for Uninsured Motorist Benefits and Underinsured Motorist Benefits. Some people mistakenly believe that by purchasing UM and UIM Benefits they are paying to provide uninsured and underinsured motorists with liability coverage. In reality, these benefits compensate you for the pain and suffering caused by uninsured motorists and by motorists whose liability coverage is insufficient to fully cover your pain and suffering. With so many uninsured and inadequately insured drivers around these days, it is not worth giving up these important coverages. Perhaps a horror story will illustrate this point.

I was recently contacted by a client who was in a serious car accident with an uninsured motorist. She assured me that she had selected the Full Tort option when her insurance came up for renewal. This led her to the mistaken impression that this selection gave her "full coverage." Unfortunately, my client had signed away her rights to Uninsured Motorist Coverage. The Full Tort selection will do her no good at all for this accident, since she has no coverage for injuries caused by uninsured motorists.

Choosing one kind of full protection does not guarantee coverage for every possible situation.

It is unfortunate that you practically need a law degree to really know what you are keeping and what you are giving up when you make each of these important selections. I advise you to consult with an attorney if you have even the least confusion. Your attorney should be willing to help, free of charge. Had my client contacted me before making her choices, I would have gladly given her five minutes of my time to ensure that she had appropriate coverage. Now it's too late.

Finally, if you are in an accident but haven't insured your car, or have waived some of your important rights, don't assume that you have no remedy. Call a personal injury lawyer for a free consultation. You have nothing to lose and maybe much to gain. There are exceptions to some of the rules set forth here. Maybe one applies to you.

OTHER COVERAGES

There are some coverages that may be worth giving up. It may be worth purchasing the minimum amount of auto insurance coverage for your medical bills if you have other health care coverage. Your health care coverage may kick in after your auto coverage is exhausted. It certainly makes no sense to pay for double coverage for the same bills. You may also have the right to give up coverages for wages you might lose because of an accident. If no one in your household is employed, it is safe to forego this coverage.

If you have an old car, it may not be cost effective to carry collision or theft coverage. Collision coverage protects you for your property damage. If you caused the accident or if you are hit by an uninsured motorist, your company will pay for your property damage (minus the deductible) if you have this coverage. If the car has little value, collision coverage has little benefit. Similarly if your old car is stolen, the insurance benefit is so minimal that it may not be worth paying for theft coverage.

"Tort Reform"—A Perspective after Five Years

Most states have passed some form of "tort reform" legislation. Now the federal government is trying to get into the act as well. While all of the statistics concerning the success of this legislation are not yet in, it is possible at this point to draw some conclusions about whether the new laws have had the intended effect.

"Tort reform" was passed into law in Pennsylvania to help bring down insurance costs by reducing the number of claims that can be brought for personal injuries. Theoretically, if insurance companies have to pay out less money towards settlement of claims, the savings will be passed along to the consumer. In fact, the Pennsylvania Legislature initially required insurance companies to roll back insurance premiums. Insurance costs have not gone down appreciably for Pennsylvania motorists in the years since "tort reform." You can judge for yourself what, if any, effect "tort reform" has had on your insurance premiums.

The perspective I can offer concerns the effect of "tort reform" on the handling of personal injury claims. Any personal injury attorney in the Philadelphia area will confirm that "tort reform" has had a dramatic impact on this area of legal practice.

For example, many smaller cases that would have been pursued prior to "tort reform" are now turned away. This is primarily because of the Limited Tort option now available in Pennsylvania. You may have a similar option in your state. Both uninsured motorists and motorists who select Limited Tort can sue for compensation only for serious injuries. While this presents a financial hardship to those who are so limited (not to mention their attorneys), it is probably a good result for society, since these smaller claims clog the system and add to insurance costs.

Claims for Uninsured Motorist Benefits are way down. UM Benefits provide compensation for the pain and suffering caused by uninsured motorists. I do not believe that the decrease in UM claims is explained by a reduction in the number of uninsured motorists in the Philadelphia area. I doubt that there are fewer uninsured motorists now than there were before the passage of the "tort reform" legislation. The reason for this decrease is that many people waive their UM coverage. Many badly injured individuals are without a legal remedy because they decided to waive UM coverage.

INSURANCE FRAUD AND OTHER PROBLEMS

11

People often wonder about the extraordinarily high cost of auto insurance, particularly in big cities. You will not be surprised to hear that there is blame to go all around. The people who bring fraudulent claims and their lawyers contribute mightily to the problem. And the doctors who knowingly over-treat plaintiffs in order to build personal injury cases are obviously at fault.

The insurance industry and its lawyers deserve a large share of the blame, too. They frequently refuse to offer fair compensation until the parties reach the courthouse steps. Insurance companies and their lawyers force extended delays before offering fair compensation while they exhaustively investigate every possible suspicion of fraud. This greatly, and often unnecessarily, increases everyone's litigation costs. Who can blame the defense for having a certain amount of skepticism? But everyone loses when the meritorious case is treated like a potential fraud. Everyone loses when reasonable settlement efforts are not made until all of the time and money has been spent preparing for trial.

The widespread public perception of fraud in personal injury cases badly hurts the average honest citizen and the reputable lawyers and doctors who work to assist them in achieving medical and financial relief from their injuries. Jurors who read in the newspaper about the allegations of fraud can be expected to return lower money verdicts when they decide personal injury cases.

There is no easy answer to the problem of insurance fraud. Stepped-up investigation by the Justice Department and state prosecutors is an important start. It is useless to hope that those responsible for the problem will voluntarily change their methods. Yet only through each individual taking care to conduct himself or herself in an honorable way can we begin to rectify this situation.

It is absolutely inexcusable for citizens, lawyers, and doctors to present anything but totally legitimate personal injury claims. If you have been injured due to the negligence of another, you need to be sure you select a lawyer and a doctor who are respected for their integrity. Otherwise prepare for a very long wait before you receive compensation for your injuries. Never forget that justice delayed may very well be justice denied.

AMBULANCE CHASERS

An accident can be a very traumatic event. An accident can leave you feeling vulnerable and at loose ends. Ambulance-chasing lawyers prey on this feeling. These lawyers, or their underlings, mysteriously pop up at the scene of accidents hoping to lure the accident victim into the web of deceit.

How do these vultures find their carrion? Some lawyers peruse police reports of auto accidents. These reports are often available for little or no charge at law enforcement agencies. They then contact the individual who appears not to have caused the accident and suggest that he or she pursue an injury claim. Several of my clients have received letters of this nature from other lawyers.

Some lawyers have people on the streets looking for accidents. It is a simple thing to buy a radio that picks up police calls. Many of my clients report being approached after an accident by one or more people who offer to take them to a lawyer's office. These people often arrive even before the police. They may have a whole system set up that at first seems attractive. They might offer to drive you to a body shop they know of, then to a hospital emergency room, and then to the lawyer's office. They might even suggest that the lawyer will lend you money.

You might be tempted to choose a lawyer who will lend you money. Resist this temptation. It is unequivocally unethical for a lawyer to lend a client money. You should select a lawyer because he or she is a good lawyer, not because he or she will lend you money. The dollars you receive up front as a loan may pale next to the small settlement you receive at the end of the case because your lawyer doesn't know what he or she doing or doesn't have your best interests at heart.

Lawyers who lend money to clients and who chase ambulances do not have your best interests in mind. They are greedy from the word go. How can you trust your legal rights to someone who practices the great profession of law in such a disreputable manner? How can you be sure that this lawyer won't lie to you when it comes time to settle your case? How can you trust that this lawyer won't sell you and your case out to avoid some extra work? You can't.

Appendix—Worksheets And Sample Forms

Car Accident Worksheet

Description of the accident:

Date of accident:

Time of day:

Day of week:

Location:

Direction in which each car was traveling:

Names, addresses and phone numbers of driver of each car:

Names, addresses and phone numbers of owner of each car:

Names, addresses and phone numbers of passengers in each car:

Names, addresses and phone numbers of all witnesses:

Number of lanes of each street:

One way or two way:

Condition of roadways:

Slope of each street:

Photographs of the scene:

Amount of traffic:

Traffic controls (lights, stop signs, etc.):

Speed of each vehicle at the time of impact and just before impact:

Length of any skid marks:

Use of brakes by each vehicle:

Use of horn by each vehicle:

Use of turn signals by each vehicle:

Point of impact on each car:

Movement of each car upon impact:

Final position of each vehicle:

License plate numbers of each vehicle:

Location of your car now:

Place where the trip began:

Destination:

Purpose of the trip:

Scheduled arrival time:

Lighting conditions:

Weather:

Use of sunglasses:

Position of the sun:

Use of alcohol/drugs by any passenger or driver:

Use of car phones:

Use of radio/car stereo:

Use of windshield wipers:

Windows open or closed:

Use of defroster:

Use of glasses/contact lenses:

Driver smoking, eating or drinking at the time of the accident:

Seat belt:

Stick shift or automatic transmission:

Last eye examination:

Name and address of eye doctor:

Date the car was purchased:

Photographs of damage to each car:

Damage done to the vehicles:

Years, makes and models:

Driver's license number:

What happened to your body at the moment of impact:

What part of your body came into contact with the vehicle:

How did you feel at the moment of impact:

Name of your insurance company:

Policy number:

Coverages:

All auto insurance in your household:

Health insurance company:

Policy number:

Coverages:

Fall Down Accident Worksheet

Description of the accident:

Names, addresses and phone numbers of all witnesses:

Date of the accident:

Time of day:

Day of week:

Location of the accident:

Condition of the accident area (e.g., sidewalk):

Photographs of the scene:

Place where the trip began:

Destination:

Purpose of the trip:

Scheduled arrival time:

Smoking, eating or drinking at the time of the accident:

Last eye examination:

Name and address of eye doctor:

Use of headphones:

Lighting conditions:

Weather:

Use of sunglasses:

Position of the sun:

Use of alcohol/drugs:

Objects carried at time of accident:

Type and condition of shoes:

All conversation at the scene:

Police district involved:

Name and badge number of officer:

What happened to your body as you fell:

What parts of your body came into contact with the ground:

How did you feel immediately after you fell:

Health insurance company:

Policy number:

Coverages:

Contingent Fee Agreement

I hereby appoint _____,

as my attorney to prosecute a claim for Personal Injuries against _____

_____, relat-

ing to injuries that occurred on _____.
                                                Date

      I hereby agree that the compensation for my attorney for services shall be determined as follows: That out of whatever sum is secured by my attorney from the above Defendant(s) by way of settlement or verdict, my attorney shall receive

        _____% thereof if my case is settled without filing a lawsuit, or

        _____% thereof if my case is settled after a lawsuit is filed, or

        _____% thereof if my case is settled after arbitration, or

        _____% thereof if my case must go to jury verdict

The expenses, including the fees of witnesses, investigation, photographs and other proper costs incurred in the preparation, trial or settlement shall be deducted before payment of my attorney's fee, and all otherwise unpaid medical expenses shall be paid from the balance remaining after payment of my attorney's fee and expenses. SHOULD NO MONEY BE RECOVERED BY SUIT OR SETTLEMENT, MY ATTORNEY SHALL HAVE NO CLAIM AGAINST ME OF ANY KIND FOR SERVICES RENDERED.

      I hereby acknowledge acceptance of this Contingent Fee Agreement.

_____   _____
        NAME

                                       _____
                                       ADDRESS

New Client Letter

Dear New Client:

I have begun processing your claim and I intend to protect your interests and achieve the maximum possible recovery. You can help assure our success by doing the following:

1. Read this letter carefully and save it for future reference.
2. DO NOT DISCUSS THIS CASE WITH ANYONE, EXCEPT FOR ME OR SOMEONE FROM MY OFFICE. REFER ALL OTHER PERSONS TO ME AND ASK YOUR FAMILY, WITNESSES AND DOCTOR TO FOLLOW THE SAME PRECAUTIONS.
3. Notify me of any change in address or telephone number.
4. Record all expenses you incur as a result of this accident and collect the bills.
5. Keep a journal of your daily pain and suffering and the effect your injury has on everyday activities and relationships. Also, inform your doctor of all symptoms so that he has accurate and complete records of your treatment.
6. Follow your doctor's advice precisely and tell me when he has finally discharged you.
7. Make a copy of your prescriptions and forward them with receipts to me.
8. Do not sign any papers concerning your claim for any insurance company, investigator or attorney.

The normal processing of a personal injury claim involves the following steps: a) The accident is investigated and necessary witness statements are secured; b) When your doctor discharges you, I collect and review all medical reports and bills, along with any record of lost earnings; c) After I carefully evaluate your case, I will attempt to negotiate an out-of-court settlement; d) I will promptly advise you of the results of the negotiations with my recommendations; and e) If no settlement can be achieved, I will institute a lawsuit on your behalf.

It is a pleasure representing you. Rest assured that your legal rights will be well protected.
Sincerely,

YOUR ATTORNEY

Authorization to Release Medical Records

You are hereby authorized and requested to furnish to _____ _____ or his representative, all my medical and drug records (including x-rays, if any), and reports, abstracts, and summaries thereof, accident and/or police reports, employment and earnings, histories and records, bills and statements, and all other information pertaining to me, to permit them to examine all originals and to make copies thereof.

_____

DATE

_____

NAME

_____

_____

ADDRESS

Opening Letter to Insurance Company

October 12, 1998

Acme Insurance Company
1300 Insurance Drive
Companytown, PA 19151
Attn: New Claims

RE: My Client: John Dough
        Your Insured: Benny Fitz
                    1234 Market Street
                    Anytown, PA 19073
        Date of Accident: 10/10/98
        Location of Accident: Broad and Market Streets, Anytown, PA

Dear Sir/Madam:

I represent John Dough in a claim for personal injuries suffered in an accident involving your insured, the particulars of which are set forth above.

Please confirm your receipt of this letter and direct all future inquiries to me.

Very truly yours,

Evan K. Aidman

EKA/sb
cc: John Dough

Opening Letter to Defendant

November 20, 1998

Rich Banks
123 Market Street
Morgantown, WV 11111

RE: My Client: I. M. Hurt
      Location of Accident: West & Main Streets, Morgantown, WV 11111
      Date of Accident: 11/16/98

Dear Mr. Banks:

I represent I.M. Hurt in a claim for personal injuries suffered in an accident in which you were involved, the particulars of which are set forth above. It is in your best interest to immediately refer this letter to your insurance company. Failure to do so will result in the institution of suit against you without further notice.

Please confirm your receipt of this letter and direct all future inquiries to me

Very truly yours

Evan K. Aidman

EKA/s

cc: I.M. Hurt

Medical Records Request

November 1, 1998

Dr. Treat M. Wright
555 Pleasant Rd.
Pleasantville, FL 33333

RE: My Client: Bro' Ken Legg
        Date of Accident: 10/16/98

Dear Dr. Wright:

I represent Bro' Ken Legg, who was injured on the above date in an accident. I understand that you have been consulted and/or are treating my client for injuries resulting from this accident.

Kindly forward to me a medical report setting forth a statement of injuries, diagnosis, treatment, prognosis and a copy of your bill to date. I am enclosing an Authorization that permits the release of this information.

Every effort will be made to protect any unpaid balance of your bill from any proceeds derived from the litigation of this matter.

Thank you for your cooperation.

Very truly yours,

EVAN K. AIDMAN

EKA/sb
Enclosure
cc: Bro' Ken Legg

Medical Records Request

May 17, 1998

Big City Hospital
111 S. 11th Street
Room 1111
Washington, D.C. 44444
Attention: Medical Records Department

RE: My Client: A. Ken Kneck
        Date of Birth: 5/19/66
        Dates of Service: 5/14/98
        Date of Accident: 5/14/98

Dear Sir/Madam:

I represent A. Ken Kneck in a claim for personal injuries arising out of an accident that occurred on the above date. It is my understanding that this patient received treatment in your hospital. Please forward a report as well as your bill for services rendered to this patient. I am enclosing a medical authorization which permits the release of this information.

Thank you for your cooperation.

Very truly yours,

F. LEE GALESE

EKA/sb
Enclosure
cc: A. Ken Kneck
    Billing Dept.

Injury and Treatment Worksheet

Injuries as a result of the accident:

Type of pain (sharp or dull, constant or intermittent):

Name and address of ambulance company:

Name and address of emergency room:

Mode of transportation to the emergency room:

Treatment at emergency room:

Medication:

Orthopedic appliances:

Arrival and departure times:

Mode of transportation home:

Condition for the rest of the day/night:

Ability to sleep:

Condition the next morning:

Ability to work:

Name, address, phone number and specialty of your family doctor:

Names, addresses, phone numbers and specialty of all doctors/therapists seen for your injuries:

Mode of transportation:

Purpose of visits:

Referral source for each doctor:

Results of first doctor visit:

Results of subsequent visits:

Description of treatments/therapy:

Exercises:

Whirlpool:

Orthopedic appliances:

Dates of treatment for each doctor/therapist:

Medication:

Date of last medical treatment:

Pain when discharged:

Medical instructions upon discharge:

Pain since discharge:

Pain today:

Surgery:

Effect of accident on your normal daily activities:

Effect on household duties:

Effect on exercise/sports:

Effect on driving:

Effect on sleeping:

Effect on social activities:

Marital difficulties:

Emotional reaction to your injuries:

Your physical/emotional condition before the accident:

Prior/subsequent accidents:

Prior/subsequent injuries:

Prior/subsequent doctors:

Next scheduled day of work after the accident:

Time missed because of the accident:

Reason for missing time:

Effect of accident on ability to work after return to your job:

Work schedule:

Average weekly wage:

Name, phone number and address of supervisor:

Questions for Depositions, Statements and Trial

Full name:

Current residence:

How long:

Residence on date of accident:

Age:

Marital status (then and now):

Children:

Employment on date of accident:

Where:

How long:

What capacity:

Duties:

Employed now:

Do you recall being involved in an accident on....:

Time of day:

Where:

Day of week:

Who was driving:

Passengers:

Where were you seated:

What happened (narrative):

What did you see:

Did you know you were going to be hit:

Lanes of street:

Amount of traffic:

Divided highway:

Parking on sides of street:

Which way do the streets run:

How fast were you traveling:

How fast was the other car traveling:

Which direction each traveling:

Turn signals:

Traffic controls:

What part of vehicles impacted each other:

What happened to your car upon impact:

Which way did vehicle spin:

Where did each stop:

What did you do after it stopped:

Where did your journey begin:

Where were you going:

Purpose of trip:

When due to arrive:

Lighting:

Weather:

Slope of street:

Alcohol/Drugs:

All conversation at the scene:

Used horn or other warning device:

Skid marks:

When did police arrive:

Conversation with police:

Who called:

Radio:

Windshield wipers:

Windows:

Defroster:

Children in car:

Last eye examination:

Do you wear glasses or contacts:

Car phone:

Smoking/eating (hands on wheel) (stick shift):

Where was the sun—sunglasses:

Witnesses:

Who owned the car:

When purchased:

Borrowed from owner:

Type of vehicle:

Where licensed to drive:

Since when:

Restrictions:

License ever suspended or revoked:

Describe other car:

Mechanical condition of your car:

Where was it last inspected:

What, if anything, happened to your body at the moment of impact:

What part of your body came into contact with the vehicle:

How did you feel at the moment of impact:

Seat belt:

Were you injured as a result of the accident:

What portion of your body came to your attention at the scene:

Investigation of accident:

What did you do about your injuries:

Emergency Room:

How got there:

Type of pain (sharp or dull, constant or intermittent):

What was done for you at ER:

Medication:

Orthopedic appliances:

When arrived at and left hospital:

How got home:

How felt rest of day:

How felt next morning:

Go back to work that day:

Did you go anywhere else for treatment:

Why:

How got there:

Purpose of visits:

Used ER equipment until first doctor's visit:

Family doctor:

Who referred:

Result of first doctor's visit:

What complained of:

What done on subsequent visits:

Describe treatments/therapy:

Exercises:

Whirlpool:

Orthopedic appliances

Where exercises performed:

Did they bring relief:

How long saw this doctor:

How many times:

How many times per week:

What other doctors saw:

Why:

Who referred:

Specialists seen:

Purpose of visits:

Medication—side effects:

When was last medical treatment:

How felt then:

How felt since then:

How feel today:

How many days a week do you feel pain—What do you do for it:

Did pain lessen at any point in treatment:

When (for each injury):

Were you ever able to resume normal daily activities:

When:

Household duties:

Sports:

Driving:

Sleeping:

Social activities:

Marital difficulties:

How felt before accident:

Prior accidents:

How long treated:

Injuries:

How long before accident had you recovered:

Later accidents:

Next scheduled work after date of accident:

Did you go:

Work schedule:

When returned to work:

Average weekly wage:

Why didn't you stay out of work:

After you went back to work, was there any limitation because of the accident:

Inability to do job:

Were you carrying anything:

Describe your shoes:

Describe your clothing:

Which foot slipped:

Describe your fall:

What parts of your body hit the ground:

What caused you to fall:

Where were you looking:

When had you last been to the scene of the accident:

Were you aware of the defect that caused your fall:

Did you have an alternate route:

Complaint—Car Accident

YOUR ATTORNEY
Identification Number 1234567   ATTORNEY FOR PLAINTIFF
24 North Lawyer Row
Bryn Mawr, PA 19010
(610) 555-1212

MANNY BUCKS   COURT OF COMMON PLEAS

                                                     CIVIL DIVISION

            v.

N. SURANCE

            and

D. POCKETS, INC.   DOCKET NUMBER: 1234567

CIVIL ACTION—PERSONAL INJURY
MOTOR VEHICLE ACCIDENT

1. Plaintiff, Manny Bucks, is an adult individual who resides at 3000 N. 7th Street, Philadelphia, PA 11111.

2. Defendant, N. Surance, is an adult individual who resides at 2000 Levick Street, Philadelphia, PA 11112.

3. Defendant, D. Pockets, Inc., is a Pennsylvania Corporation with an address for service of process at 123 Wister Street, Philadelphia, PA 11113.

4. On or about January 6, 1997, at approximately 5:00 p.m., plaintiff, Manny Bucks, was operating a motor vehicle in a northerly direction on Whitaker Avenue at or near its intersection with Roosevelt Boulevard in the City and County of Philadelphia, Commonwealth of Pennsylvania.

5. At the aforesaid time, date and place, defendant, N. Surance, was operating a motor vehicle on Roosevelt Boulevard at or near the said intersection when, suddenly and without warning, defendant side swiped plaintiff's motor vehicle.

6. The plaintiff did not own a motor vehicle at the time of the accident, nor did he reside in a household in which a motor vehicle was insured.

7. The Full Tort option applies to plaintiff, and he is therefore eligible to receive compensation from defendant without regard to the severity of his injury.

8. The said accident was caused solely through the negligence of the defendants and was due in no manner whatsoever to any actions taken by the plaintiff.

9. At all relevant times, defendant, N. Surance, acted as the agent, servant, workman and/or employee of defendant, D. Pockets, Inc., and/or in the alternative acted on his own behalf, and was acting within the course and scope of his authority.

10. The negligence of the defendants consisted of the following:
a. Operating the motor vehicle at a high and excessive rate of speed;
b. Failing to have the said motor vehicle under proper and adequate control at the time;
c. Failing to give proper and sufficient warning of the approach of the said vehicle;
d. Operating the said vehicle without due regard for the rights, safety and position of the plaintiff at the point aforesaid;
e. Violating the various ordinances of the City of Philadelphia and the statutes of the Commonwealth of Pennsylvania pertaining to the operation of motor vehicles;
f. With plaintiff's motor vehicle in plain view, failing to exercise care and vigilance so as to avoid the collision;

11. Solely as the result of the defendants' negligence, the plaintiff sustained severe personal injuries to his head, body, and limbs; more particularly, he suffered: post-traumatic cervical sprain and strain, post-traumatic headaches, lumbosacral strain, shock and injury to his nerves and nervous system, and he was otherwise injured.

12. All the above injuries are serious and permanent except those of a superficial nature. All of the foregoing injuries have rendered the plaintiff, sick, sore, lame, prostrate, disabled and disordered and have made him undergo great mental anguish and physical pain, as a result of which he has suffered, yet suffers, and will continue to suffer for an indefinite time in the future.

13. As a further result of this accident, plaintiff may in the future continue to suffer great pain and agony and he may be prevented from attending to his usual daily work and occupation to his great financial damage and loss.

WHEREFORE, plaintiff, Manny Bucks, demands judgment against defendants, N. Surance and D. Pockets, Inc. in an amount not in excess of FIFTY THOUSAND ($50,000.00) DOLLARS, plus costs of this suit.

_____
YOUR ATTORNEY
Attorney for Plaintiff

Complaint—Fall Down Accidents

YOUR ATTORNEY
Identification Number 2345678   ATTORNEY FOR PLAINTIFF
26 Little River Turnpike
Alexandria, VA 22222
(703) 555-1212

C. Ewan Court   COURT OF COMMON PLEAS
and
D. Vorce Court   CIVIL DIVISION

      v.

U.R. Richman, Inc.

                        DOCKET NUMBER: 9876543

CIVIL ACTION—PERSONAL INJURY

PREMISES LIABILITY, SLIP AND FALL

     1. Plaintiff, C. Ewan Court is an adult individual who resides at 123 Apple St., Annandale, VA 22333.

     2. Plaintiff, D. Vorce Court is the wife of Plaintiff, C. Ewan Court, and she resides at 123 Apple St., Annandale, VA 22333.

     3. Defendant, U.R. Richman, Inc., is a business entity licensed to do business in the Commonwealth of Virginia with an address for service of process at 200 Curtis Avenue, Alexandria, VA 22335.

     4. On or about January 25, 1998, at approximately 11:15 A.M. and for a long time prior thereto, there existed a patch of ice in the parking lot of the defendant's grocery store located at 6000 North Broad Street, in Alexandria, which presented a substantial impediment to travel.

     5. The defendant knew or should have known of the said patch of ice in the parking lot, and the fact that it presented a substantial impediment to travel sufficiently prior to the said time and date to take such action as would cure the said condition.

     6. On the date and time aforesaid, defendant had under its care and direction the supervision, control and maintenance of the said property and had the duty to keep it free from snow and ice and safe for travel for those lawfully traversing the said area.

7. On the date and time aforesaid, plaintiff, C. Ewan Court was lawfully traversing the said area, at which time he slipped and fell to the ground after he stepped onto the said patch of ice, thereby sustaining certain injuries which are hereafter more particularly set forth.

8. The said accident was the result of the defendant's negligence, and was due in no manner whatsoever to any act or failure to act on the part of the plaintiffs.

9. The negligence of the defendant consisted of the following:

(a)   Allowing a patch of ice to remain in the said area;

(b)   Failing to make the said area safe for travel for those lawfully upon the said premises;

(c)   Failing to maintain the said area in a condition that would protect and safeguard persons lawfully entering the area;

(d)   Failing to have the said area inspected at reasonable intervals in order to determine its condition;

(e)   Failing to warn persons lawfully traversing the said area of the dangerous condition of such;

(f)   Disregarding the rights and safety of plaintiff, C. Ewan Court at the time he was traversing the said area;

(g)   Violating the codes and ordinances of the City of Alexandria and the statutes of the Commonwealth of Virginia pertaining to property maintenance and condition of public walkways;

(h)   Otherwise failing to use due care under the circumstances, as well may be pointed out during the discovery and trial phases of this matter;

(i)   Directing plaintiff, C. Ewan Court to park his car directly next to the said patch of ice;

(j)   Failing to spread rock salt, dirt or any other substance on the said parking lot in order to make it safe for guests of the defendant's grocery store.

COUNT I

10. The allegations contained in paragraphs 1 through 9 above are incorporated by reference as though set forth in full.

11. Solely as the result of the defendant's negligence, plaintiff, C. Ewan Court sustained severe personal injuries to his head, body, and limbs; more particularly, he suffered: right distal fibula fracture, right knee abrasions, shock and injury to his nerves and nervous system, and he was otherwise injured.

12. All the above injuries are serious and permanent except those of a superficial nature. All of the foregoing injuries have rendered plaintiff, C. Ewan Court sick, sore, lame, prostrate, disabled and disordered and have made him undergo great mental anguish and physical pain, as a result of which he has suffered, yet suffers, and will continue to suffer for an indefinite time in the future.

13. As a further result of this accident, plaintiff, C. Ewan Court may in the future continue to suffer great pain and agony and he may be prevented from attending to his usual daily work and occupation to his great financial damage and loss.

14. As a further result of this accident, plaintiff, C. Ewan Court has suffered an injury which is in full or part a cosmetic disfigurement which may be permanent, irreparable and severe.

15. As a further result of this accident, plaintiff, C. Ewan Court has suffered other financial losses which are hereby claimed from the defendant.

WHEREFORE, plaintiff, C. Ewan Court demands judgment against the defendant, in an amount in excess of FIFTY THOUSAND ($50,000.00) DOLLARS, plus costs of this suit.

COUNT II

16. The allegations contained in paragraphs 1 through 15 above are incorporated by reference as though set forth in full.

17. Solely as a result of the foregoing negligence of the defendant, plaintiff, D. Vorce Court, has been deprived of the aid, comfort, assistance, society, companionship and services of her husband, and she may be deprived of the same in the future, all of which is to her great damage and financial loss.

18. As a further result of this accident, plaintiff, D. Vorce Court has been or will be obliged to expend various sums of money or to incur various expenses resulting from the aforementioned injuries suffered by plaintiff, C. Ewan Court and she may be obliged to continue to expend such sums or incur such expenditures for an indefinite time in the future.

WHEREFORE, plaintiff, D. Vorce Court demands judgment in her favor and against defendant, in an amount in excess of FIFTY THOUSAND ($50,000.00) DOLLARS, plus costs.

_____
YOUR ATTORNEY
Attorney for Plaintiffs

Request for Production of Documents

YOUR ATTORNEY   ATTORNEY FOR PLAINTIFF
Identification Number 1234567
24 North Lawyer Row
Bryn Mawr, PA 19010-3045
(610) 555-1212

LEAH BILITY   COURT OF COMMON PLEAS

                                                     CIVIL DIVISION

    v.

SUE PREAM COURT   DOCKET NUMBER: 3333333
and
ARTHUR DAVIT

REQUEST FOR PRODUCTION OF DOCUMENTS

       Plaintiff hereby requests, pursuant to Pennsylvania Rule of Civil Procedure 4009, that the defendants produce the documents I hereinafter request in accordance with the definitions and instructions contained herein within thirty (30) days after service of this request, at the offices of the undersigned and permit the undersigned to inspect and copy these documents.

       1. All photographs, records, films, charts, sketches, graphs and diagrams of the area involved in this accident or occurrence, the locale or surrounding area of this accident or occurrence, or any other matter or thing involved in this accident or occurrence taken and/or prepared.

       2. All statements, memoranda or writings (signed or unsigned) of any and all witnesses including any and all statements, memoranda, or writings of plaintiff and/or defendants and/or all persons involved in this accident or occurrence. The statements referred to herein are defined by Pennsylvania Rule of Civil Procedure 4003.4.

       3. All transcripts and summaries of all interviews conducted by anyone on behalf of defendants of any potential witness or person who has any knowledge of the accident or its surrounding circumstances.

       4. All interoffice memoranda between representatives of defendants or memoranda to defendants' file concerning the manner in which the accident occurred.

       5. All interoffice memoranda between representatives of defendants or memoranda to defendants' file concerning the injuries you sustained.

6. A copy of any written accident report concerning this accident or occurrence signed by or prepared by defendants.

7. Any and all copies of reports, correspondence, memoranda and writings rendered by any expert witness employed or consulted by defendants and/or anyone acting on defendants' behalf concerning this case.

8. The entire claims and investigation file or files of the defendants, defendants' counsel, or any other organization, excluding references to mental impressions, conclusions or opinions representing the value or merit of the claim or defense or respecting strategy or tactics and privileged communication from counsel.

9. All property damage estimates rendered for any object belonging to you and/or defendants that was involved in this accident or occurrence.

10. Any and all documents containing the names and home and business addresses of all individuals contacted as potential witnesses.

11. Any and all press releases in the possession of defendants' counsel.

BY:_____
          YOUR ATTORNEY
          Attorney for Plaintiff

Client Letter: Independent Medical Examination

Dear Client:

      I am sending you this letter to give you some helpful instructions concerning the medical examination to be conducted by the doctor chosen by the insurance company. You need to be aware that this doctor is paid by the insurance company. If possible, he will make medical findings that are favorable to the insurance company and unfavorable to you. That will help to ensure that he receives future assignments from the insurance company. In other words, this doctor is not on your side.

      Therefore, it is important that you follow the instructions contained in this letter carefully. Please be sure to wear a watch to the examination. You need to time the actual physical examination. When the doctor actually begins physically examining you, check your watch. When the physical examination is complete, check your watch again. Please call me and let me know exactly how long this examination took. The initial part of the exam where you are asked about the accident and your medical history are not part of the physical examination. Only begin timing the exam when the doctor actually begins his tests.

      If the doctor asks you to do something that hurts, by all means let the doctor know that it hurts. If you fail to do this, the doctor will put down that you are fine when in fact you may have pain. Do not let the doctor push you further than you comfortably can go. However, do not unnecessarily resist. The doctor will know if you are attempting to resist and this will look very bad in the medical report. Do not say something hurts if it does not. The doctor will know if you are being dishonest.

      Even though this doctor is not your friend, you should be courteous and pleasant at all times. The doctor is simply doing his job, and you will not help yourself by becoming hostile in any way.

      You are not absolutely required to have x-rays if you have recently had x-rays taken. You can let the doctor know that you have just had x-rays and that you would prefer not to be x-rayed again.

      You do not have to wait forever for the doctor. If the examination does not begin within 20 minutes of your scheduled arrival time, let the receptionist know that you will have to leave if the examination does not begin within 10 minutes. After 10 minutes, if the examination has not yet begun, let them know that you have to go and then, if you wish, leave.

      Do not get into specifics about the accident. You can speak very generally about what happened to you but do not get into too many details. You can tell the doctor to contact me for more details. It is a good idea to answer questions about the accident as briefly as possible.

      Finally, watch out for tricks. Sometimes doctors will drop an object to see if the patient bends over to pick it up. If the patient claims that he cannot bend over and then manages to bend over to pick up the object, the doctor will note this in his report.

      Please call me immediately after the examination so that we can discuss how it went. Feel free to call me before the exam if you have any questions.

                    Sincerely,

                    Your Attorney

Interrogatories—Car Accident

YOUR ATTORNEY
Identification Number 1234567   ATTORNEY FOR PLAINTIFFS
24 North Lawyer Row
Bryn Mawr, PA 19010-3045
(610) 555-1212

WARREN PEACE   COURT OF COMMON PLEAS
    and
SUE U. DALEY   CIVIL DIVISION
    v.
NOAH FAULT   DOCKET NUMBER: 200000

INTERROGATORIES
ADDRESSED TO DEFENDANT

Demand is hereby made that you answer the following interrogatories under oath or verification pursuant to the Pa. R.C.P. No. 4005 and 4006 within thirty (30) days from service hereof. The answering party is under a duty to supplement their responses under the following conditions:

The party must supplement his response with respect to any question, directly addressed to the identity and location of persons having knowledge of discoverable matters and the identity of each person expected to be called as an expert witness at trial.

A party or expert witness must amend a prior response if he obtains information upon the basis of which:

(a) he knows that the response was incorrect when made; or,

(b) he knows that the response, though correct when made, is no longer true.

I. DEFINITIONS

The following definitions are usage that apply to all of the Interrogatories contained herein:

A.   The singular and masculine form of any noun or pronoun shall embrace, and be read and applied as, the plural or feminine or neuter as circumstances may make appropriate.

B.   "Document" refers to all types of written, recorded or graphic matter, however produced or reproduced.

C.   "Person" refers to any person, firm, corporation, partnership, proprietorship, association or agency.

D.   "Plaintiff" refers to you in this matter.

E.   "Identify" when used:

1.   In reference to a person, means to state the full name, full title, last known resident address, last known business address and last known occupation and business affiliation.

2.   In reference to documents, means to state with respect to each and every document, the type of document, author's name, recipient's name, date of preparation, present or last known custodian and location, and title and identification code or number of the file in which the document is kept.

II.   INTERROGATORIES

1.   State:

   (a)   Your name, age, date and place of birth;

   (b)   Any other name by which you have ever been known;

   (c)   Your present address and your address at the time of the accident;

   (d)   Your marital status at the time of the accident;

   (e)   Your present marital status;

   (f)   Your Social Security number;

   (g)   Whether you are a licensed driver and, if so, where and when you were first licensed;

   (h)   Any and all restrictions on your driver's license at the time of the accident and at present;

   (i)   Your operator's license number;

   (j)   Whether you have any physical defects, and if so, their nature and duration;

   (k)   Whether you had taken any medication within the 24 hours preceding the accident. If yes, identify the medication and the condition for which it was taken;

   (l)   Whether you had taken any other drugs, within the 24 hours preceding the accident. If yes, identify the drugs so taken;

   (m)   Whether you had consumed any alcoholic beverages within the 8 hours preceding the accident. If yes, state when, what type of alcoholic beverage, where you consumed it and how much you consumed;

(n) Whether you were under the care of a physician, psychiatrist or psychologist at the time of the accident and, if so, the name and address of the physician, psychiatrist or psychologist;

(o) Whether or not you have ever been convicted of a crime of moral turpitude or *crimen falsi,* and if so, please state the county, court, term, number and charges;

(p) Whether you ever served in the Armed Forces. If so, state the date, branch, rank at discharge, any infirmities at discharge, any claims made and any benefits received for infirmities, and your Veteran's Administration Claim Number.

CIRCUMSTANCES SURROUNDING THE ACCIDENT

2. State the date, time and exact location of the accident.

3. With reference to the trip you were taking at the time of the accident herein, state:

(a) Where it started;

(b) When it started;

(c) Where it was scheduled to end;

(d) The route followed to the accident scene and any stops made along the way;

(e) The purpose of the trip;

4. Did you have passengers in your vehicle at the time of the accident? If so, state:

(a) Their names and addresses;

(b) Their relationship to you; and

(c) Where they were located in your vehicle at the time of the accident;

5. State as to the motor vehicle involved in the accident:

(a) The make, model and year;

(b) The serial number;

(c) The mileage at the time of the accident;

(d) Whether it had previously been in any accidents, indicating the date thereof and the parts damaged;

(e) The type of brakes, their condition and the date they were last repaired or adjusted;

    (f) Whether the horn was in operating condition and when it was last used before the accident;

    (g) Whether the windows were open or closed and whether you were able to see through them clearly.

6. As to the road on which your vehicle was being operated at the time of the accident, state:

    (a) The type of road surface, i.e., concrete, blacktop, etc.

    (b) The surface condition, i.e., dry, wet, muddy, etc.;

    (c) Whether there were any defects in the road. If so, describe the same;

    (d) Whether the road was a one-way or a two-way street;

    (e) The number of lanes;

    (f) Whether the road was a divided highway;

    (g) Whether any buildings were located on either side of the road;

    (h) Whether there was any road construction, and if so, describe the same;

    (i) The grade of the road;

    (j) The straightness or curve of the road;

    (k) The lighting conditions at the time of the accident.

7. State:

    (a) The weather conditions prevailing at the time of the accident;

    (b) The exact intersection or highway where the accident occurred;

    (c) The position of all vehicles at the time of the accident;

    (d) The distance from you when you first observed the other vehicle and/or vehicles;

    (e) When and where you applied your brakes;

    (f) The distance traveled between the point when the brakes were applied and the point of impact;

    (g) An estimate of the respective speeds of the vehicles at the time of impact;

    (h) The initial point of impact for each vehicle.

8. Describe how the accident occurred, including the actions of the respective parties and particularly detail any action you took to avoid the accident.

9. At what point in time did you first realize that the accident was going to occur?

10. State the name and address of the owner or owners of the motor vehicle you operated or occupied at the time of the accident.

11. State whether or not you were acting on behalf of your employer or in the course of your employment at the time of the accident referred to in the Complaint.

12. Did your vehicle carry any cargo and/or loads? If so, describe:

   (a) What the cargo or the load was; and

   (b) Its location in the vehicle.

13. Do you wear glasses or contact lenses? If so, state:

   (a) Whether you were wearing them at the time of the accident:

   (b) As accurately as you can, the condition for which they were prescribed;

   (c) Your visual acuity without glasses; and

   (d) Your visual acuity with glasses.

14. State:

   (a) Whether there were any obstructions in your view when approaching the scene of the accident, and, if so, please describe each such obstruction in detail, giving its location with relation to the site of the accident;

   (b) Whether at the time of the accident your vision was impaired or obscured in any manner, either from inside of the vehicle or from external factors and, if so, in what manner your vision was impaired or obscured.

15. State whether or not prior to the time of the accident you had traveled the road upon which the accident occurred. If so, please state the frequency and the last time that you traveled the road prior to the accident.

16. Where were you looking just prior to the time of the accident?

17. State where the point of impact was, giving the distance in feet with reference to the nearest intersection and/or other established points.

18. Describe the movement of your motor vehicle within the last 30 seconds immediately prior to the occurrence.

19. State whether you gave any warning of your approach. If so, state in detail the nature of the said warning.

20. Describe all physical evidence, including its location, which you observed at the scene of the accident after the collision, including but not limited to dirt, debris, etc.

21. State whether any skid marks were made by any vehicle involved in the accident. If so, state as to each vehicle:

     (a) The length and direction of the said skid marks;

     (b) The point of beginning and ending of the said skid marks.

22. State the type and color of any traffic signal controlling the street on which your vehicle was traveling when you first noticed it and:

     (a) The distance in feet the traffic light was from the vehicle at the time;

     (b) Whether or not the signal had changed between the time you first observed it and the accident;

     (c) If the light did change, from what color to what color did it change;

     (d) The exact location of all traffic signals.

23. At or immediately following the time of the accident, was there any conversation relevant to the accident or injuries sustained which you engaged in or heard? If yes, state:

     (a) The identity of the speaker;

     (b) The substance of what was said;

     (c) The identity of all persons within hearing distance.

24. State how all the parties involved in the accident were removed from the accident, including the name, address, present whereabouts and job classification of all persons assisting in their removal.

25. State whether the accident was caused by any broken, defective or unworkable device, or by the breaking, absence, misplacement or malfunction of any equipment, or of any similar condition. If so, state:

     (a) The particular things involved and the precise nature of the defect;

     (b) When the defect first arose;

     (c) What caused the defect;

     (d) When you learned of the defect for the first time;

     (e) If the said defect existed prior to the accident, state how long it existed prior thereto;

     (f) What, if anything, was done to remedy this defect after the accident?

PROPERTY DAMAGE

26. State the condition of your vehicle at the time of the accident, describing specifically any damage which existed prior to the accident.

27. When and where was that vehicle last inspected prior to the accident in question and what, if any, repairs were made or parts replaced at the time of inspection?

28. Describe specifically what parts of your vehicle were damaged in the accident, listing the damage to each of those parts.

29. Did you obtain estimates for the repairs of these damages? If so, give the names and addresses of the repair shops and the amounts of the estimates.

30. If the damages were repaired, state:

    (a) The date or dates on which repairs were made;

    (b) The name and address of the person who made the repairs;

    (c) The total cost of repairs.

31. Please attach a copy of all repair bills or estimates.

32. State whether any damage to property other than the motor vehicles involved resulted from the accident, and if so, describe such damage.

INJURIES RELATING TO THE ACCIDENT

33. State in detail all injuries you sustained in the accident or as a result thereof.

34. Have you contacted anyone regarding injuries sustained by any other party in this action? If so, state the name of such persons and the substance of any information received from said person.

35. State whether you saw either plaintiff subsequent to this accident in question and, if your answer is in the affirmative, set forth:

    (a) The date you saw either plaintiff;

    (b) The places at which you saw either plaintiff; and

    (c) The identity and condition of the plaintiff at this time.

WITNESSES AND THOSE WITH KNOWLEDGE OF THE ACCIDENT

36. State the names and addresses of all persons who you or anyone acting on your behalf, including but not limited to attorneys and insurance adjusters, know or believe:

    (a) Actually witnessed the accident:

    (b) Were present at the scene of the accident immediately after its occurrence;

    (c) Were within sight or hearing of the accident.

STATEMENTS

37. Please state the nature of any oral statements made by either plaintiff concerning the occurrence. Please state when, where and to whom the statements were made.

38. Have you or anyone acting on your behalf obtained from any person any statement (as defined by the Rules of Civil Procedure) concerning this action or its subject matter?

If so:

    (a) State the names and addresses of each such person;

    (b) State when, where, by whom and to whom each statement was made, and whether it was reduced to writing or otherwise recorded;

    (c) State the names and addresses of each person who has custody of any such statements that were reduced to writing or otherwise recorded;

    (d) Attach a copy of each such statements to these Interrogatories.

39. Do you have knowledge of any transcript or of testimony in any proceeding arising out of the occurrence? If so, please identify it.

STATEMENTS MADE BY PARTY TO WHOM INTERROGATORY IS ADDRESSED

40. Have you given any statement as defined by the Rules of Civil Procedure concerning this action or its subject matter?
If so, please:

    (a) State the names and addresses of each person to whom a statement was given;

    (b) State when and where each statement was given;

(c) State the names and addresses of each person who has custody of any such statements that were reduced to writing or otherwise recorded.

(d) Attach a copy of each such statement to these Interrogatories.

DEMONSTRATIVE EVIDENCE

41. Are you or anyone in your behalf in possession of maps, models, plans, diagrams or drawings relating to the accident complained of, showing the locale or surrounding area of the site of the accident or any other matters involved in the accident? If so, attach a copy of said map, plan or diagrams to these Interrogatories and state:

(a) The date(s) when such maps, models, plans, diagrams or drawings were taken or made and what they are;

(b) The names and addresses of the person or persons taking or making the same;

(c) The subject that each represents or portrays;

(d) The name, address and job classification of the person having possession or custody of the same.

42. Are you or anyone acting in your behalf, including but not limited to attorneys and insurance adjusters, in possession of any photographs, motion pictures or video recordings relating to the accident complained of, showing the local or surrounding area of the site of the accident or any other matters or things involved in the accident? If so, attach a copy and state:

(a) The dates when such photographs, motion pictures or video recordings were taken or made;

(b) The names, addresses and job classifications of the person or persons taking the same;

(c) The subject that each represents or portrays;

(d) What location each was taken from;

(e) The name, address and job classification of the person having possession or custody of the same.

TRIAL PREPARATION MATERIAL

43. Have you or anyone on your behalf, including but not limited to attorneys and insurance adjusters, conducted any investigation of the accident which is the subject matter of the complaint?

If the answer is in the affirmative, please:

(a) State the names and addresses of each such person, and the employer of each person, who conducted any investigations;

(b) State the subject matter of the investigation;

(c) State the dates of the investigation;

(d) Describe all notes, reports, or other documents prepared during or as a result of the investigations and the identity of the persons who have possession thereof;

(e) Attach copies of any and all documents, memoranda, notes, photographs and statements obtained as a result of the investigation.

EXPERTS

44. Identify by name and address any experts with whom you have consulted who will not be called upon to testify.

45. Identify by name and address any experts with whom you have consulted who will be called upon to testify at trial.

46. As to the experts in question No. 45 state:

(a) The background and qualifications of each said expert, listing the schools attended, years of attendance, degrees received, and experience in any particular field of specialization or expertise;

(b) The subject matter upon which each expert will testify;

(c) The substance of all the facts and all the opinions to which each expert will testify;

(d) The grounds for each expert's opinion.

INSURANCE

47. State whether you are covered by any type of insurance, including any excess or umbrella insurance, in connection with this accident;

If the answer is affirmative, state the following with respect to each policy:

(a) The name of the insurance carrier(s) that issued each policy of insurance;

(b) The named insured under each policy and the policy number;

(c) The type of each policy and the effective dates;

(d) The amount of coverage provided for injury to each person, for each occurrence, and in the aggregate for each policy;

(e) Each exclusion, if any, in the policy which is applicable to any claim thereunder and the reasons why you or the company claims the exclusion is applicable;

(f) Whether you have made a claim under the policy and if so, set forth the nature of the claim, the amount recovered and the date of recovery;

48. Did you make an oral or written report or give any other notice of the accident to any insurance company or agent or broker? If so:

(a) State if the report was written or oral;

(b) Please attach copies and/or transcriptions of said reports.

49. State whether or not any insurer has a file on the accident herein and, if so where the file is located.

50. Did you receive any compensation from, or make a claim under any Workers' Compensation Insurance Plans as a result of the accident in question? If your answer is in the affirmative, please state:
(a) The name of the insurance company or companies providing such coverage;

(b) The date of the claim and the policy or claim number involved;

(c) The name of the insurance adjuster or supervisor handling the claim and his office address;

(d) If any claim was disallowed, please state the specific nature of the claim made and the reason(s) given by the insurance company for the denial.

51. Identify and give the home and business addresses of all witnesses who you anticipate will testify at the trial of this matter.

52. If you are not the registered owner of the motor vehicle you were driving at the time of the accident, state by what authority you were driving the said motor vehicle.

53. Were you performing any duties or acts on behalf of any person or entity other than yourself at the time of the accident?

54. If the answer to the preceding interrogatory is yes, state the name, home address and business address of each such person and/or entity.

55. Identify and give the home and business addresses of all persons having knowledge of any discoverable matters.

_____   BY: _____
Attorney for Defendant   YOUR ATTORNEY
                                                                       Attorney for Plaintiff

Interrogatories—Fall Down Accident

YOUR ATTORNEY
Identification Number 1234567   ATTORNEY FOR PLAINTIFF
24 North Lawyer Row
Bryn Mawr, PA 19010-3045
(610) 359-1919

AXEL DENT   COURT OF COMMON PLEAS
        v.   CIVIL DIVISION
D. FENDANT   DOCKET NUMBER: 123456789

PLAINTIFF'S INTERROGATORIES ADDRESSED TO DEFENDANT

Demand is hereby made that you answer the following interrogatories under oath or verification pursuant to the Pa. R.C.P. No. 4005 and 4006 within thirty (30) days from service hereof. The answering party is under a duty to supplement his responses under the following conditions:

The party must supplement his response with respect to any question, directly addressed to the identity and location of persons having knowledge of discoverable matters and the identity of each person expected to be called as an expert witness at trial.

A party or expert witness must amend a prior response if he obtains information upon the basis of which:

(a) he knows that the response was incorrect when made; or,

(b) he knows that the response, though correct when made, is no longer true.

I. DEFINITIONS

The following definitions are usage that apply to all of the Interrogatories contained herein:

A. The singular and masculine form of any noun or pronoun shall embrace, and be read and applied as, the plural or feminine or neuter as circumstances may make appropriate.

B. "Document" refers to all types of written, recorded or graphic matter, however produced or reproduced.

C. "Person" refers to any person, firm, corporation, partnership, proprietorship, association or agency.

D. "Plaintiff" refers to the plaintiff in this matter.

E. "Identify" when used:

1. In reference to a person, means to state the full name, full title, last known resident address, last known business address and last known occupation and business affiliation.

2. In reference to documents, means to state with respect to each and every document, the type of document, author's name, recipient's name, date of preparation, present or last known custodian and location, and title and identification code or number of the file in which the document is kept.

II. INTERROGATORIES

1. Were you aware, prior to the filing of the Complaint in this action, that plaintiff was injured while on the premises made reference to in the Complaint?

2. Did you receive notice of this accident from the plaintiff?

If so, state:

(a) The date, time and place you received the notice;

(b) Whether this was written or oral and if written, the name and address of the person who now has custody of it.

3. Did you receive notice of the accident from any other person?

If so, state:

(a) The date, time and place you received the notice;

(b) The name, address and telephone number of the person from whom you received the notice;

(c) Whether the notice was written or oral, and if written, the name and address of the person who now has custody of it.

4. If you will do so without a Motion to Produce, attach a copy of each written notice to your answers to these Interrogatories.

5. What is the name and address of each person who, on the date of the accident, was the owner of the real property located at the premises made reference to in the Complaint?

6. What was the nature and extent of each person's ownership interest?

7. What financial interest did each owner of the real property have in the said premises?

8. Were the premises made reference to in the Complaint subject to any lease on the date of the accident? If so, state the name and address of the lessors, lessees and sublessees.

9. What is the name and address of each person who managed and controlled these premises on the date of the accident?

For each such person, state:

(a) His job title;

    (b) A description of his duties;

    (c) What his financial interest in these premises is;

    (d) The inclusive dates of his management up until the present time;

    (e) A description of his qualifications and experience in managing such a business;

    (f) The name and address of each other business at which he has been employed, and the inclusive dates of such employment.

10. State the name, address and job title of the person who was in charge of these premises at the time plaintiff was injured:

11. Where was such person located at the time of the accident?

12. Was any person responsible for supervising the area in which plaintiff was injured at the time of the accident?

If so, for each person state:

    (a) His name and address;

    (b) His job title;

    (c) A description of his duties;

    (d) His location at the time of the accident.

13. Were there any employees on these premises, or other person, on duty at the time of the accident?

If so, for each such person state:

    (a) His name and address:

    (b) His job title;

    (c) A description of his duties;

    (d) His location at the time of the accident.

14. Does the area of the premises where the accident occurred have a particular designation?

If so, what is the designation?

15. Describe the accident site.

16. Was there a defect or collection of debris in the area where the accident is alleged to have occurred?

If so, for each collection of debris or defect, give a description of it;

17.   If you will do so without a Motion to Produce, attach a copy of each written complaint, warning or other notice with regard to the area of the premises where the accident occurred.

18.   Were inspections made prior to the accident to determine whether the area where the plaintiff was injured was in a safe condition for use by workers or other occupants of the area?

If so, state:

(a)   The frequency of such inspections;

(b)   The date and time of the last inspection prior to the accident;

(c)   The name, address, and job title of the person who made the last inspection;

(d)   The substance of the findings that were made on the last inspection;

(e)   Whether any instructions were given as a result of the last inspection to remove, clean or alter anything in the area of the accident, and, if so, a description of the instructions, and the name of each person to whom such instructions were given.

19.   Was any inspection made of the scene of the accident subsequent to the accident?

If so, state:

(a)   The date and time it was made;

(b)   The name, address and job title of each person who made the inspection;

(c)   What findings were made.

20.   Did you, or any employee, receive any complaint, warning or other notice, concerning a dangerous or defective condition on the premises prior to the accident?

If so, for each complaint, warning or other notice, state:

(a)   The date and time it was received;

(b)   Whether it was written or oral and, if oral, the substance of it;

(c)   The name or other means of identification and address of the person by whom it was given;

(d)   The name, address and job title of the person who received it;

(e)   The nature and location of the danger or defect to which it related;

(f)   Whether any action was taken as a result of it, and if so, a description of the action, and the time at which it was taken.

21. Was any warning given to plaintiff or any other person concerning any danger in the area where the accident occurred?

     If so, for each warning state:

     (a) The warning that was given;

     (b) The name or other means of identification and address of the person who gave the warning;

     (c) The name or other means of identification and address of each person to whom it was given;

     (d) The form in which it was given;

     (e) The reason it was given.

22. Was there any guardrail, sign or other marking in the area where the accident occurred?

     If so, for each such marking, state:

     (a) A description of it;

     (b) Its location;

     (c) Its purpose;

     (d) Whether it was in use at the time of the accident, and if not, the reason it was not in use.

23. Has any other accident occurred on your premises in the same area as, or in a similar manner to the accident in which plaintiff was injured?

     If so, for each accident, state:

     (a) The date and time it occurred:

     (b) A description of how it occurred;

     (c) The name, or other means of identification, and address of the person to whom it occurred;

     (d) The location in which it occurred;

     (e) Whether any safety precaution was taken as a result of it, and if so, a description of such safety precaution.

24. Was any repair or alteration made subsequent to the accident in the area where plaintiff was injured?

     If so, for each repair or alteration, state:

     (a) A description of it:

(b) The date it was made;

(c) The name, address and occupation of the person who made it;

(d) The reason it was made.

25. Was an investigation made by you, or in your behalf, as a result of the accident?

If so, for each investigation, state:

(a) The date it was made;

(b) The name, address and occupation of each person who made it;

(c) Whether any report was made of it, and if so, the name and address of the person who has custody of the report.

26. If you will do so without a Motion to Produce, attach a copy of each investigation report to your answers to these interrogatories.

27. Did you or any employee make a report of the accident?

If so, for each report, state:

(a) The name, address and job title of the person who made it;

(b) The date and time it was made:

(c) The name and address of the person to whom it was made;

(d) Whether written or oral, and, if written, the name and address of the person who has custody of it.

28. Did you receive a report of the accident from the plaintiff or any other person?

If so, for each person, state:

(a) His name and address;

(b) The date and time he made the report;

(c) The name, address and job title of the person to whom he made the report;

(d) Whether he made a written or oral report, and if written, the name and address of the person who has custody of the report.

29. If you will do so without a Motion to Produce, attach a copy of each written report concerning the accident to your answers to these interrogatories.

30. Do you contend that plaintiff was not authorized to be on that part of the premises where the accident occurred?

If so, on what facts do you base such contention?

31. Do you contend that plaintiff was guilty of contributory negligence?

If so, on what facts do you base such contention?

32. Do you contend that plaintiff assumed the risk of the accident?

If so, on what facts do you base such contention?

33. Was there a policy of insurance that covered you on the date of the accident against the type of risk here involved?

If so, for each policy, state:

(a) The name and address of the insurer;

(b) The number of the policy;

(c) The effective date thereof;

(d) The nature of the coverage;

(e) The limits of liability;

(f) The name and address of the custodian of the policy.

34. Do you have, or know of the existence of, any photograph or diagrams relating to any matter concerning this accident?

If so, for each photograph or diagram, state:

(a) A description of what it depicts;

(b) The name, address and occupation of the person who took or made it;

(c) The date, time and place it was taken or made;

(d) The name and address of the person who has custody of it.

35. If you will do so without a Motion to Produce, attach a copy, at the expense of the plaintiff, of each photograph or diagram to your answers to these Interrogatories.

36. Were any statements obtained by you, or on your behalf, from any person concerning the accident?

If so, for each statement identify:

(a) The name, address, occupation and name of employer of the person who made it;

(b) The name, address and occupation of the person who obtained it;

(c) The date and time it was obtained;

(d) Whether written or oral, and if written, the name and address of the person who has custody of it.

37. If you will do so without a Motion to Produce, attach a copy of each written statement to your answers to these Interrogatories.

38. State the name, home address and business address of the following persons:

(a) All persons known to defendant or its representatives who witnessed the accident forming the basis of this claim;

(b) All persons who came to the scene of the accident following the occurrence;

(c) All persons who were within sight or hearing of the accident at the time it occurred but who did not actually witness it.

(d) All persons having relevant knowledge concerning the happening of the accident and the cause therefor.

39. Have you or anyone acting on your behalf, obtained a written or oral statement from the plaintiff? If so, for each and every such statement, set forth:

(a) The name and address of the person who obtained the statement;

(b) The date of the statement;

(c) Was it written or oral;

(d) If oral, whether it was recorded or transcribed;

(e) The name and address of the person who presently has custody of the statement or recording thereof.

40. Have you made any statement as defined in Pa. R.C.P. 4003.4 to any person concerning the accident? If so, for each and every such statement, set forth:

(a) The date of each statement;

(b) Whether written or oral;

(c) If oral, whether recorded or transcribed;

(d) The name and address of the person who obtained each statement;

(e) The name and address of the person presently having custody of each statement or recording thereof.

41. Have you or anyone acting on your behalf obtained any written or oral statements as defined in Pa. R.C.P. 4003.4 from any person who has knowledge of the happening of the accident, whether as an actual witness or as a pre-accident or a post-accident witness? If so, for each and every statement, set forth:

(a) The name and address of the person from whom each statement was obtained;

(b) The date of each statement;

(c) Whether each statement was written or oral;

(d) If oral, whether each statement was recorded or transcribed;

(e) The name and address of the person(s) who obtained each statement;

(f) The name and address of the person(s) who presently has custody of each statement or recording thereof.

42. State whether or not defendant or his representatives, other than his attorney, has possession of any written or typed and/or recorded memorandum which contains factual data obtained by them from interviews or discussions with any person who has knowledge of the happening of the accident. If so, for each and every such memorandum, set forth:

(a) The date of the memorandum;

(b) The name and address of the person who composed the memorandum;

(c) The name and address of the person who presently has custody of the memorandum.

43. State whether you, your representative, your attorney or any other person to your knowledge caused to be made or now has any photographs, motion pictures, charts, diagrams, graphs or recordings depicting or concerning the scene of the accident or the parties involved in the accident. If so, set forth the name and address of each and every person who presently has custody and describe the contents of such photographs, motion pictures, charts, diagrams, graphs and/or recordings.

44. At the time of the accident, was defendant covered by one or more insurance policies providing coverage for liability in excess of the applicable basic policy, including but not limited to, any personal or family coverage, excess coverage, "umbrella" policy, "catastrophe" policy, or any such additional coverage? If so, as to such policy, state the following:

(a) The name of the carrier issuing the policy;

(b) The amount of coverage provided.

45. Does defendant, its representatives or anyone acting in its behalf, other than its attorney, have in its possession a report concerning the plaintiff which was obtained from a credit bureau and/or insurance index system of claimants and/or a casualty, health or life insurance company? If so, please state:

(a) From whom such report was obtained, setting forth the name of the organization and its last known address;

(b) The date which report was obtained;

(c) The name, last known address and job title of the person and/or persons presently in possession of same.

46. Identify by name and address each and every person whom you expect to call as an expert witness at the trial of this claim. As to each witness, state:

(a) The subject matter on which he is expected to testify;

(b) The facts and opinions to which he is expected to testify;

(c) A summary of the grounds for each opinion;

(d) Whether the facts and opinions listed in (b) above are contained in a written report, memorandum or other transcript, and if they are, give the name and address of the present custodian of same and state whether you will produce the same without the necessity of a Motion;

(e) If the opinion of any expert listed above is based in whole or part on any scientific rule or principal, set forth the said rule or principal;

(f) If the opinion of any expert listed above is based in whole or in part on any code, regulation or standard and specifically set forth the section relied upon;

(g) If the opinion of any expert listed above is based in whole or in part upon any scientific or engineering textbook or other publication, identify said text or publication;

(h) If the expert has testified in court or by way of oral deposition within the past ten years, describe the court involved, set forth the caption of the case, the date of testimony and the name and address of the attorney calling said expert as a witness.

47. With respect to each person you expect to call as an expert witness at the trial of this matter, state:

(a) His age, residence and business address;

(b) The name and address of his present employer, or if self-employed, the name and address of the business and his occupation;

(c) The name and address of every person or firm who employed the expert for the last ten years and a detailed description of all duties at each place of employment. If the expert was self-employed, state specifically and in detail the description of his duties and responsibilities;

(d) His education background, specifying colleges attended, dates of attendance, degrees attained and in a detailed list of all writings prepared by the expert or in which the expert participated in any way whatsoever.

48. Did the defendant, its attorney or anyone acting on its behalf receive any notices, reports or complaints during a one-year period prior to the accident from any source or whatsoever concerning or relating to the condition of the area set forth above? If so, please state:

    (a) The name and address of the author;

    (b) The nature of each such notice, report or complaint;

49. State whether or not, and in particular how often, periodic inspections and/or examinations were made of the area set forth above during a one-year period immediately preceding the date of the accident involved herein and since the date of the accident.

50. Describe the inspections made of the area referred to above just before and just after the accident, setting forth the names, addresses and job classifications of each person or persons making such inspections.

51. Identify the location of any written or typed reports made of the inspections referred to in the preceding interrogatory.

52. State what physical cracks and/or holes and/or defects were discovered, if any, by the aforesaid inspection.

53. With regard to the defendant, please state the name, last known address, present whereabouts, if known, of the following persons:

    (a) President;

    (b) Vice President;

    (c) Treasurer;

    (d) Secretary;

    (e) Security Personnel;

    (f) Counter Person.

54. Please state the last known address and present whereabouts, if known, of all of defendant's employees who were on duty at the time of plaintiff's accident.

55. Identify and give the home and business addresses of all lay witnesses who you anticipate will testify at the trial of this matter, and state the subject on which he is to testify.

56. Identify and give the home and business addresses of all persons having knowledge of any discoverable matters.

57. If you have conducted any surveillance of plaintiff or any other person relevant to this litigation, state:

    (a) Time and date of surveillance;

    (b) Method used;

(c) Name, business address, telephone number, employer of person taking this surveillance;

(d) Name, address, telephone number of the custodian of the medium used to record such surveillance.

58. Identify with particularity all persons, animals or vehicles involved in the occurrence, either directly or indirectly, and explain such involvement.

59. Explain in detail your version of how the occurrence happened, if you feel that it is not completely covered in your answers above.

_____

YOUR ATTORNEY
Attorney for Plaintiff

Motion to Compel Discovery

YOUR ATTORNEY
Identification Number 1234567   ATTORNEY FOR PLAINTIFF
24 North Lawyer Row
Bryn Mawr, PA 19010-3045
(610) 555-1212

IMA PLAINTIFF   COURT OF COMMON PLEAS

v.   CIVIL DIVISION

D. SCUVRY   DOCKET NUMBER: 35791113

MOTION TO COMPEL DISCOVERY

Plaintiff, by undersigned counsel, hereby moves the Court to enter an Order pursuant to PA. R. C. P. 4019 compelling defendant, D. Scuvry, to answer certain discovery propounded by plaintiff in this matter.

In support of this Motion, plaintiff avers as follows:
1. On November 3, 1997, plaintiff served Interrogatories and Requests for Production of Documents upon counsel for defendant by first class mail.
2. Pursuant to PA. R. C. P. 4006(a)(2), defendant's answers and objections to the said Interrogatories and Requests were due on or before December 3, 1997.
3. Plaintiff requires an Order of this Court pursuant to PA. R. C. P. 4019(a)(1)(i) compelling defendant to answer the said Interrogatories and to respond to the said Requests for Production of Documents.

WHEREFORE, plaintiff respectfully requests the Court to enter an Order compelling defendant to file full and complete answers to plaintiff's Interrogatories and documents responsive to Plaintiff's Request for Production or suffer appropriate sanctions to be imposed upon application to the Court.

_____
IMA LAWYER, ESQUIRE
Attorney for Plaintiff

Order for Discovery

YOUR ATTORNEY
Identification Number 1234567   ATTORNEY FOR PLAINTIFF
24 North Lawyer Row
Bryn Mawr, PA 19010-3045
(610) 555-1212

IMA PLAINTIFF   COURT OF COMMON PLEAS

v.   CIVIL DIVISION

JERRY TRIAL   DOCKET NUMBER: 35791113

ORDER

　　　　AND NOW, this day of _____, 19____, upon consideration of plaintiff's Motion to Compel Discovery, it is hereby ORDERED that the said Motion is GRANTED. Defendant, Jerry Trial, shall answer plaintiff's Interrogatories and respond to plaintiff's Request for Production of Documents within twenty (20) days of the date of this Order or appropriate sanctions shall be imposed upon defendants following application to the Court. All documents produced or withheld are to be numbered consecutively beginning with the number one.

　　　　　　　　　　　　　　　　BY THE COURT:

　　　　　　　　　　　　　　　　_____

　　　　　　　　　　　　　　　　　　　　　　　J.

Voir Dire Questions

YOUR ATTORNEY
Identification Number 1234567   ATTORNEY FOR PLAINTIFFS
24 North Lawyer Row
Bryn Mawr, PA 19010-3045
(610) 555-1212

RICK CHASER   COURT OF COMMON PLEAS
   and
N. TARA GATORESE   CIVIL DIVISION
   v.
CITY OF PHILADELPHIA   DOCKET NUMBER: 7654321

VOIR DIRE QUESTIONS

A. Attorneys and Parties

1. Does anyone on this jury panel know me?

2. Do any of you know Lit. E. Gator, who represents the defendant, City of Philadelphia or anyone from the Office of the City Solicitor?

3. Does anyone on this panel know either of my clients, Rick Chaser and N. Tara Gatorese?

4. Does anyone know these potential witnesses: Jerry Verdict, Lee Ding Questions or C.U. Fall?

B. Personal

5. Can you each tell me your current marital status?

6. Are any of you or your immediate families employed by a company engaged in the casualty or liability insurance business?

7. Are any of you or your immediate families stockholders in any company which, in whole or in part, is engaged in the casualty or liability insurance company?

8. Are any of you or your immediate families now employed, or have any of you or your immediate families ever been employed, as a claims adjuster or otherwise by a company or concern which, in whole or in part, was engaged in the casualty or liability insurance business?

9. Are any of you or your immediate families now employed, or have any of you or your immediate families ever been employed by the City of Philadelphia?

10. Can I ask each of you to tell me the type of work in which you and your spouse, if you are married, are at present involved and for how long?

11. Have any of you, or has any member of your family, ever been involved in a auto accident which resulted in the filing of any type of claim, either by or against you or some member of your family?

12. Have any of you ever been on a jury which tried an auto accident? When?

13. Have any of you ever sat on a jury panel in any kind of case? Type of case? When?

14. Most people know the facts must be proven beyond a reasonable doubt in criminal cases. Does everyone understand and accept that this is a civil case where facts are proven by a preponderance of the evidence which is not nearly as strict as a test as beyond a reasonable doubt, and requires much less evidence? In other words, does everyone understand that the test is not beyond a reasonable doubt, but rather "more likely than not"?

C. Attitudes

15. Is there anyone on this panel who feels that a person injured by someone else's conduct should not sue for monetary compensation as a result of those injuries?

16. How many in this room feel that persons injured in an accident as a result of the negligence of another person should just bear his/her own losses and pain and suffering?

17. Has anyone here or any members of their families or any close acquaintance ever been sued? If so, did you feel that lawsuit against you was unjustified? Would the fact that you were sued make it difficult for you to sit as a fair and impartial juror in this case?

18.   Is there anyone here who has any feelings for any reason against persons claiming money damages in personal injury cases?

19. Is there anyone among the panel who believes that there are too many personal injury lawsuits?

20. Is there anyone on this panel who, for religious or any other reason, does not believe in medicine, in doctors, or that a person may require professional medical treatment for physical pain and suffering?

D. Damages

21. How many in this room have any personal convictions, or fixed opinions, or religious beliefs that might make it difficult for you to award substantial compensation to these plaintiffs for the injuries they suffered, if the evidence during this trial supports such damages?

22. Do you agree that the size of the award you may make in this case should be in proportion to the seriousness of the injuries proven during the trial?

23. Have any of you ever been involved in, or is there now pending, either by you or against you, any litigation growing out of a civil action for negligence and in particular, with regard to personal injuries?

24. Can each of you make a commitment to me that you will pay close attention to and fully consider and calculate the value of each element of damages on which His Honor the Judge instructs you at the end of this trial in reaching

your verdict rather than just selecting an amount of money that feels as if it should be enough regardless of the evidence and the instructions, assuming the evidence will support a verdict for the plaintiffs?

25. Does anyone disagree with the concept that the City of Philadelphia has the same status as any other defendant and that it has duties and obligations which may render it legally responsible if it fails to fulfill those obligations?

26. Would anyone have difficulty returning a verdict against the City of Philadelphia if you felt that it had failed to fulfill the obligations imposed on it by law?

E. General

27. Is there any reason whatever, why any member of this panel cannot sit and listen to the evidence in this case for several days, paying close and careful attention to it? Any reason, whether physical, or any other, why any of you cannot do that?

28. As you know, each party to a lawsuit is entitled to have his or her case tried by an unbiased and impartial jury, free from all prejudices or influences that would affect the decision. An attorney for any of the parties has a duty to his client to see to it that such a jury is selected, and this is my purpose in these questions. It is not my purpose to pry into your private life or to cause you embarrassment, but only to secure for my clients the fair trial to which they are entitled. I, therefore, ask you whether any of you know of any other matter, anything which I have not covered in my questions, which would for any reason influence you or prevent you from rendering a fair and impartial verdict in the case?

29. Is there any reason whatever, whether I have mentioned it or not, why any of you feel you cannot be fair and impartial jurors in this case?

30. Is there any member of the panel who would, for any reason whatsoever, prefer not to sit on this jury?

Respectfully submitted,

_____

IMA LAWYER
Attorney for Plaintiffs

Jury Instructions

YOUR ATTORNEY
Identification Number 1234567
24 North Lawyer Row
Bryn Mawr, PA 19010-3045
(610) 555-1212

ATTORNEY FOR PLAINTIFFS

B. YONDA SCOPE
   and
MEL PRACTICE
     v.
CITY OF PHILADELPHIA

COURT OF COMMON PLEAS

CIVIL DIVISION

DOCKET NUMBER: 7654321

POINTS FOR CHARGE

DIRECTED VERDICT

1.   Upon consideration of all of the evidence and the law applicable to this case, I hereby direct you to return a verdict in favor of plaintiffs, B. Yonda Scope and Mel Practice, and against defendant, City of Philadelphia.

DUTY OF CARE

2.   Defendant's duty of protection and care to plaintiffs, on April 30, 1998, was the highest duty required by the law since the plaintiffs were invited visitors of the defendant at the time of this accident. *Treadway v. Ebert Motor Company*, 463 A. 2d 994, 998 (Pa. Super. 1981).

Defendant was under an affirmative duty on April 30, 1998, to protect the plaintiffs not only against danger which its employees knew about, but also against those which with reasonable care one or more of its employees might have discovered. *Treadway v. Ebert Motor Company*, 463 A. 2d 994, 998 (Pa. Super. 1981).

Plaintiffs entered the Philadelphia City Hall on April 30, 1998, with the City of Philadelphia's implied assurance of preparation and reasonable care for their protection and safety while they were there. *Treadway v. Ebert Motor Company*, 463 A. 2d 994, 998 (Pa. Super. 1981).

DUTY TO WARN

3.   Defendant had an affirmative duty to warn the plaintiffs of any defects on the floor surface, which were either known to the City of Philadelphia or its employees or which were discoverable by reasonable inspection. *Greco v. 7-Up Bottling Co.*, 165 A. 2d 5 (Pa. 1960).

Defendant had an affirmative duty to warn the plaintiffs of any failure to maintain the school premises in a reasonably safe condition and the plaintiffs were entitled to rely on the City's performance of this duty. *Bersa v. Great Atlantic & Pacific Tea Company,* 215 A. 2d 289, 292 (Pa. Super. 1965).

NEGLIGENCE

4.   The legal term negligence, otherwise known as carelessness, is the absence of ordinary care which a reasonably prudent person would exercise in the circumstances here presented. Negligent conduct may consist either of an act or an omission to act when there is a duty to do so. In other words, negligence is the failure to do something which a reasonably careful person would do, or the doing of something which a reasonably careful person would not do, in light of all the surrounding circumstances established by the evidence in this case. It is for you to determine how a reasonably careful person would act in those circumstances. Pa. S.S.J.I. (Civ.) 3.01.

VICARIOUS LIABILITY

5.   The defendant, City of Philadelphia, as an employer, is liable for any negligent acts or failures to act of its employees. Pa. S.S.J.I. (Civ.) 4.04. I instruct you that William Anderson and Donna Johnson are employees of the defendant and, as such, the defendant is legally responsible for any of their negligent acts or failures to act.

NOTICE

6.   You must find that the defendant was negligent if you believe that the evidence has shown that the defendant, in the exercise of reasonable care, ought to have known of the existence of the water before the accident. *Moultrey v. Great Atlantic & Pacific Tea Company*, 422 A. 2d 593, 596 (Pa. Super. 1980).

Defendant is chargeable with constructive notice of a defective condition which exists for such a period of time that in the normal course of events, this condition would have come to its attention. *Green v. Prise*, 404 Pa. 71, 170 A. 2d 318 (1991).

PROOF OF NOTICE

7.   The Plaintiffs can establish that defendant ought to have known of the existence of the water either by direct or circumstantial evidence. *Moultrey v. Great Atlantic and Pacific Tea Company,* 422 A.2d 593, 594 (Pa. Super. 1980).

CIRCUMSTANTIAL EVIDENCE

8.   Circumstantial evidence consists of proof of facts, or circumstances, from which it is reasonable to infer the existence of another fact. You may consider circumstantial evidence and you should give it whatever weight you believe it deserves. Pa. S.S.J.I. (Civ.) 5.07.

PROOF

9.   Plaintiffs need not exclude every reasonable possibility that could have caused the accident; it is not necessary that every fact or circumstance point to liability, but it is enough that there be sufficient facts for you to say that by a preponderance of the evidence, liability is favored. *Swartz v. General Electric Co.,* Pa. Super. 474 A.2d 1172 (1984).

PRECISION OF PROOF

10. The Plaintiffs are not required to prove the precise manner in which the water came to be on the floor, nor are they required to prove with mathematical exactness that the accident could only happen in one manner to the exclusion of all other possibilities. *Finney v. G.C. Murphy Co.,* 178 A.2d 719 (Pa. 1902).

ASSUMPTION OF RISK

11. You may not find that the plaintiffs assumed the risk of their injuries unless you find that with appreciation and knowledge of an obvious danger, they purposely elected to abandon a position of relative safety and chose to move to a place of obvious danger and by reason of the repositioning were injured. *McIntyre v. Cusick,* 372 A.2d 864, 866 (Pa. Super. 1977).

You may not find the plaintiffs assumed this risk unless you also find that they were subjectively aware of the facts which created the danger and that they appreciated the danger itself and the nature, character and extent which made it unreasonable. *Crance v. Sohanic,* 496 2d 1230, 1232 (Pa. Super. 1985).

You may not find that the plaintiffs assumed the risk unless you also find that they fully understood the risks involved in walking over water and that they voluntarily chose to encounter these risks under circumstances manifesting a willingness to accept the risk. *Fish v. Gosnell,* 463 A.2d 1042, 1048 (Pa. Super. 1983).

Since the evidence has shown that the plaintiffs were not aware of the danger presented by the water, I instruct you to find that they did not assume the risk of their injuries.

CONFLICT OF TESTIMONY

12. You may find inconsistencies in the evidence. Even actual contradictions in the testimony of witnesses do not necessarily mean that any witness has been willfully false. Poor memory is not uncommon. Sometimes a witness forgets; sometimes he remembers incorrectly. It is also true that two persons witnessing an incident may see or hear it differently.

If different parts of the testimony of any witness or witnesses appear to be inconsistent, you the jury should try to reconcile the conflicting statements, whether of the same or different witnesses, and you should do so if it can be done fairly and satisfactorily.

If, however, you decide that there is a genuine and irreconcilable conflict of testimony, it is your function and duty to determine which, if any, of the contradictory statements you will believe. Pa. S.S.J.I. (Civ.) 5.04.

REAL PROPERTY EXCEPTION TO THE P.S.T.C.A.

13. You may return a verdict in favor of the plaintiffs and against the defendant if you find that the accident involves the care, custody or control of real property of the City of Philadelphia. 42 P. S. Section 8542 (b)(3). I instruct you to return such a finding if you conclude that the defendant failed to provide sufficient matting protection to ensure safe entrance into the Philadelphia City Hall. *Singer v. City of Philadelphia,* 513 A.2d 1108, 1109-10(Pa. Cmwlth. 1986).

MONEY DAMAGES

14. If you find that the defendant is liable to plaintiffs, you must then find an amount of money damages which you believe will fairly and adequately compensate each of them for all physical and financial injuries they each sustained as a result of the accident. The amount which you award today must compensate them completely for damage sustained in the past, as well as damage they will sustain in the future. Pa. S.S.J.I. (Civ.) 6.00.

PERMANENT LOSS OF A BODILY FUNCTION

15. In order for the plaintiffs to be entitled to recover for their pain and suffering, you must find that they suffered a permanent loss of a bodily function. You may rely on their testimony and that of the doctors who testified in reaching this finding.

PAST PAIN AND SUFFERING

16. If you find that B. Yonda Scope has suffered a permanent loss of a bodily function, she is entitled to be fairly and adequately compensated for such physical pain, mental anguish, discomfort, inconvenience and distress as you find she has endured from the time of the accident until today. Pa. S.S.J.I. (Civ.) 6.01E.

FUTURE PAIN AND SUFFERING

17.   If you find that she has suffered a permanent loss of a bodily function, B. Yonda Scope is further entitled to be fairly and adequately compensated for such physical pain, mental anguish, discomfort, inconvenience and distress as you believe she will endure in the future as a result of her injuries. Pa. S.S.J.I. (Civ.) 6.01F.

LOSS OF EARNINGS AND EARNING CAPACITY

18. B. Yonda Scope is entitled to be fairly and adequately compensated for the past, present and future loss of her earnings and earning capacity. This aspect of damages is awardable whether or not you find that she has suffered a permanent loss of a bodily function. 42 P. S. Section 8553 (c)(1).

MEDICAL BILLS

19. B. Yonda Scope is entitled to be fairly and adequately compensated for all outstanding costs of the medical diagnosis, treatment and care required by the injuries suffered in this accident, and she is also entitled to compensation for all such future costs which may be incurred because of those injuries. Pa. S.S.J.I. (Civ.) 6.01A. You do not need to find that she has suffered a permanent loss of a bodily function in order for her to recover her past and future medical costs. Those costs are recoverable without regard to the permanency of the injury she suffered. 42 P.S. Section 8553 (c)(3). The only item of damages that depends upon a finding of permanency is for B. Yonda Scope's pain and suffering. Each of the other elements of damage is recoverable whether she suffered a permanent injury or not.

PROOF OF DAMAGES

20. The fact that the precise amount of damages which B. Yonda Scope has suffered or will suffer may be difficult to ascertain does not affect her right to recover those damages or your right to award them. Although you may not render a verdict based upon mere speculation or guesswork, the law allows B. Yonda Scope reasonable leeway in her method and proof of damages, so long as there is a reasonable basis in the evidence for you to estimate what her damages have been and likely will be. *Starlings v. Ski Round Top Corporation,* 493 F. Supp. 507 (M.D. Pa. 1980); *Weinglass v. Gibson,* 304 Pa. 203, 207 (1931).

Respectfully submitted,

_____

YOUR ATTORNEY
Attorney for Plaintiffs

General Release

KNOW ALL MEN BY THESE PRESENTS that I, D. Rick Testimonee, for and in consideration of the payment to us of $10,500.00 and other good and valuable consideration, have remised, released, quitclaimed and forever discharged and by these presents do, for myself, my heirs, executors, and administrators remise, release, quitclaim and forever discharge Manny and Les Bucks and Acme Insurance Company their heirs, executors, administrators, successors and assigns, and all of them, of and from all actions, causes of action, demands, damages, costs, loss of services, expenses, compensation and all consequential damage arising out of or in any way growing out of any and all personal injuries resulting or to result from an incident that occurred on or about November 1, 1997, at or near Ridge Avenue and Glennwood Avenue, Birmingham, AL. IN WITNESS WHEREOF, I have hereunto set my hand and seal this 12th day of January, 1998.

_____(SEAL)
                    D. RICK TESTIMONEE

INDEX

Your #1 Source for Real World Legal Information...

LEGAL SURVIVAL GUIDES™

- Written by lawyers
- Simple English explanation of the law
- Forms and instructions included

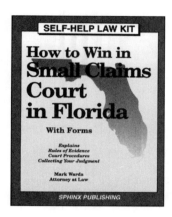

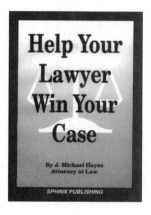

HOW TO WIN IN SMALL CLAIMS COURT IN FLORIDA

This book discusses such matters as filing a case, defending a lawsuit, settling, presenting a case, countersuing and cross-claiming against a third party, expert witnesses, the rules of evidence, and collecting a judgement. Also available for NY and TX.

123 pages; $14.95;
ISBN 0-913825-97-2

VICTIMS' RIGHTS

The financial loss from crime can devastate the victim and his or her family. Medical and psychological treatment costs can far exceed any property loss. Now, crime victims anywhere in the U.S. can find out how to obtain compensation for these losses.

163 pages; $12.95;
ISBN 0-913825-82-4

HELP YOUR LAWYER WIN YOUR CASE

Even with a lawyer, what you know may determine whether you win or lose, and how much it will cost you. This book shows you how to save money, and help win your case. Topics include: selecting a lawyer, giving your lawyer good information, asking the right questions, understanding the system, and helping your lawyer prepare your case.

156 pages; $12.95;
ISBN 1-57248-021-1

What our customers say about our books:

"It couldn't be more clear for the lay person." —R.D.

"I want you to know I really appreciate your book. It has saved me a lot of time and money." —L.T.

"Your real estate contracts book has saved me nearly $12,000.00 in closing costs over the past year." —A.B.

"...many of the legal questions that I have had over the years were answered clearly and concisely through your plain English interpretation of the law." —C.E.H.

"If there weren't people out there like you I'd be lost. You have the best books of this type out there." —S.B.

"...your forms and directions are easy to follow." —C.V.M.

Legal Survival Guides are directly available from the publisher, or from your local bookstores.
For credit card orders call 1–800–43–BRIGHT, write P.O. Box 372, Naperville, IL 60566,
or fax 630-961-2168

LEGAL SURVIVAL GUIDES™ NATIONAL TITLES
Valid in All 50 States

LEGAL SURVIVAL IN BUSINESS

How to Form Your Own Corporation (2E)	$19.95
How to Register Your Own Copyright (2E)	$19.95
How to Register Your Own Trademark (2E)	$19.95
Most Valuable Business Forms You'll Ever Need	$19.95
Most Valuable Corporate Forms You'll Ever Need	$24.95
Software Law (with diskette)	$29.95

LEGAL SURVIVAL IN COURT

Crime Victim's Guide to Justice	$19.95
Debtors' Rights (2E)	$12.95
Defend Yourself Against Criminal Charges	$19.95
Grandparents' Rights	$19.95
Help Your Lawyer Win Your Case	$12.95
Jurors' Rights	$9.95
Legal Malpractice and Other Claims Against Your Lawyer	$18.95
Legal Research Made Easy	$14.95
Simple Ways to Protect Yourself From Lawsuits	$24.95
Victim's Rights	$12.95
Winning Your Personal Injury Claim	$19.95

LEGAL SURVIVAL IN REAL ESTATE

How to Buy a Condominium or Townhome	$16.95
How to Negotiate Real Estate Contracts (2E)	$16.95
How to Negotiate Real Estate Leases (2E)	$16.95
Successful Real Estate Brokerage Management	$19.95

LEGAL SURVIVAL IN PERSONAL AFFAIRS

How to File Your Own Bankruptcy (4E)	$19.95
How to File Your Own Divorce (3E)	$19.95
How to Make Your Own Will	$12.95
How to Write Your Own Living Will	$9.95
Living Trusts and Simple Ways to Avoid Probate	$19.95
Neighbor vs. Neighbor	$12.95
Power of Attorney Handbook (2E)	$19.95
Social Security Benefits Handbook	$14.95
U.S.A. Immigration Guide (2E)	$19.95
Guia de Inmigracion a Estados Unidos	$19.95

Legal Survival Guides are directly available from the publisher, or from your local bookstores.

For credit card orders call 1–800–43–BRIGHT, write P.O. Box 372, Naperville, IL 60566, or fax 630-961-2168

Legal Survival Guides™ State Titles
Up-to-date for Your State

New York

How to File for Divorce in NY	$19.95
How to Make a NY Will	$12.95
How to Start a Business in NY	$16.95
How to Win in Small Claims Court in NY	$14.95
Landlord's Rights and Duties in NY	$19.95
New York Power of Attorney Handbook	$12.95

Pennsylvania

How to File for Divorce in PA	$19.95
How to Make a PA Will	$12.95
How to Start a Business in PA	$16.95
Landlord's Rights and Duties in PA	$19.95

Florida

Florida Power of Attorney Handbook	$9.95
How to Change Your Name in FL (3E)	$14.95
How to File a FL Construction Lien (2E)	$19.95
How to File a Guardianship in FL	$19.95
How to File for Divorce in FL (4E)	$21.95
How to Form a Nonprofit Corp in FL (3E)	$19.95
How to Form a Simple Corp in FL (3E)	$19.95
How to Make a FL Will (4E)	$9.95
How to Modify Your FL Divorce Judgement (3E)	$22.95
How to Probate an Estate in FL (2E)	$24.95
How to Start a Business in FL (4E)	$16.95
How to Win in Small Claims Court in FL (5E)	$14.95
Land Trusts in FL (4E)	$24.95
Landlord's Rights and Duties in FL (6E)	$19.95
Women's Legal Rights in FL	$19.95

Georgia

How to File for Divorce in GA (2E)	$19.95
How to Make a GA Will (2E)	$9.95
How to Start and Run a GA Business (2E)	$18.95

Illinois

How to File for Divorce in IL	$19.95
How to Make an IL Will	$9.95
How to Start a Business in IL	$16.95

Massachusetts

How to File for Divorce in MA	$19.95
How to Make a MA Will	$9.95
How to Probate an Estate in MA	$19.95
How to Start a Business in MA	$16.95
Landlord's Rights and Duties in MA	$19.95

Michigan

How to File for Divorce in MI	$19.95
How to Make a MI Will	$9.95
How to Start a Business in MI	$16.95

Minnesota

How to File for Divorce in MN	$19.95
How to Form a Simple Corporation in MN	$19.95
How to Make a MN Will	$9.95
How to Start a Business in MN	$16.95

North Carolina

How to File for Divorce in NC	$19.95
How to Make a NC Will	$9.95
How to Start a Business in NC	$16.95

Texas

How to File for Divorce in TX	$19.95
How to Form a Simple Corporation in TX	$19.95
How to Make a TX Will	$9.95
How to Probate an Estate in TX	$19.95
How to Start a Business in TX	$16.95
How to Win in Small Claims Court in TX	$14.95
Landlord's Rights and Duties in TX	$19.95

Legal Survival Guides are directly available from the publisher, or from your local bookstores.

For credit card orders call 1–800–43–BRIGHT, write P.O. Box 372, Naperville, IL 60566, or fax 630-961-2168

Legal Survival Guides™ • Order Form

Qty	ISBN	Title	Retail
	Legal Survival Guides Fall 97 National Frontlist		
	1-57071-223-9	How to File Your Own Bankruptcy (4E)	$19.95
	1-57071-224-7	How to File Your Own Divorce (3E)	$19.95
	1-57071-227-1	How to Form Your Own Corporation (2E)	$19.95
	1-57071-228-X	How to Make Your Own Will	$12.95
	1-57071-225-5	How to Register Your Own Copyright (2E)	$19.95
	1-57071-226-3	How to Register Your Own Trademark (2E)	$19.95
	Fall 97 New York Frontlist		
	1-57071-184-4	How to File for Divorce in NY	$19.95
	1-57071-183-6	How to Make a NY Will	$12.95
	1-57071-185-2	How to Start a Business in NY	$16.95
	1-57071-187-9	How to Win in Small Claims Court in NY	$14.95
	1-57071-186-0	Landlord's Rights and Duties in NY	$19.95
	1-57071-188-7	New York Power of Attorney Handbook	$12.95
	Fall 97 Pennsylvania Frontlist		
	1-57071-177-1	How to File for Divorce in PA	$19.95
	1-57071-176-3	How to Make a PA Will	$12.95
	1-57071-178-X	How to Start a Business in PA	$16.95
	1-57071-179-8	Landlord's Rights and Duties in PA	$19.95
	Legal Survival Guides National Backlist		
	1-57071-166-6	Crime Victim's Guide to Justice	$19.95
	1-57248-023-8	Debtors' Rights (2E)	$12.95
	1-57071-162-3	Defend Yourself Against Criminal Charges	$19.95
	1-57248-001-7	Grandparents' Rights	$19.95
	0-913825-99-9	Guia de Inmigracion a Estados Unidos	$19.95
	1-57248-021-1	Help Your Lawyer Win Your Case	$12.95
	1-57071-164-X	How to Buy a Condominium or Townhome	$16.95
	1-57248-035-1	How to Negotiate Real Estate Contracts (2E)	$16.95
	1-57248-036-X	How to Negotiate Real Estate Leases (2E)	$16.95
	1-57071-167-4	How to Write Your Own Living Will	$9.95
	1-57248-031-9	Jurors' Rights	$9.95
	1-57248-032-7	Legal Malpractice and Other Claims Against Your Lawyer	$18.95
	1-57248-008-4	Legal Research Made Easy	$14.95
	1-57248-019-X	Living Trusts and Simple Ways to Avoid Probate	$19.95
	1-57248-022-X	Most Valuable Business Forms You'll Ever Need	$19.95
	1-57248-007-6	Most Valuable Corporate Forms You'll Ever Need	$24.95
	0-913825-41-7	Neighbor vs. Neighbor	$12.95
	1-57248-044-0	Power of Attorney Handbook (2E)	$19.95
	1-57248-020-3	Simple Ways to Protect Yourself From Lawsuits	$24.95
	1-57248-033-5	Social Security Benefits Handbook	$14.95
	1-57071-163-1	Software Law (w/diskette)	$29.95
	0-913825-86-7	Successful Real Estate Brokerage Mgmt.	$19.95
	1-57248-000-9	U.S.A. Immigration Guide (2E)	$19.95
	0-913825-82-4	Victim's Rights	$12.95
	1-57071-165-8	Winning Your Personal Injury Claim	$19.95
	Florida Backlist		
	0-913825-81-6	Florida Power of Attorney Handbook	$9.95
	1-57248-028-9	How to Change Your Name in FL (3E)	$14.95
	0-913825-84-0	How to File a FL Construction Lien (2E)	$19.95
	0-913825-53-0	How to File a Guardianship in FL	$19.95
	1-57248-046-7	How to File for Divorce in FL (4E)	$21.95

Qty	ISBN	Title	Retail
	Florida Backlist (cont')		
	1-57248-004-1	How to Form a Nonprofit Corp in FL (3E)	$19.95
	0-913825-96-4	How to Form a Simple Corp in FL (3E)	$19.95
	1-57248-027-0	How to Make a FL Will (4E)	$9.95
	1-57248-056-4	How to Modify Your FL Divorce Judgement (3E)	$22.95
	1-57248-003-3	How to Probate an Estate in FL (2E)	$24.95
	1-57248-005-X	How to Start a Business in FL (4E)	$16.95
	0-913825-97-2	How to Win in Small Claims Court in FL (5E)	$14.95
	1-57248-029-7	Land Trusts in FL (4E)	$24.95
	1-57248-057-2	Landlord's Rights and Duties in FL (6E)	$19.95
	0-913825-73-5	Women's Legal Rights in FL	$19.95
	Georgia Backlist		
	1-57248-058-0	How to File for Divorce in GA (2E)	$19.95
	1-57248-047-5	How to Make a GA Will (2E)	$9.95
	1-57248-026-2	How to Start and Run a GA Business (2E)	$18.95
	Illinois Backlist		
	1-57248-042-4	How to File for Divorce in IL	$19.95
	1-57248-043-2	How to Make an IL Will	$9.95
	1-57248-041-6	How to Start a Business in IL	$16.95
	Massachusetts Backlist		
	1-57248-051-3	How to File for Divorce in MA	$19.95
	1-57248-050-5	How to Make a MA Will	$9.95
	1-57248-053-X	How to Probate an Estate in MA	$19.95
	1-57248-054-8	How to Start a Business in MA	$16.95
	1-57248-055-6	Landlord's Rights and Duties in MA	$19.95
	Michigan Backlist		
	1-57248-014-9	How to File for Divorce in MI	$19.95
	1-57248-015-7	How to Make a MI Will	$9.95
	1-57248-013-0	How to Start a Business in MI	$16.95
	Minnesota Backlist		
	1-57248-039-4	How to File for Divorce in MN	$19.95
	1-57248-040-8	How to Form a Simple Corporation in MN	$19.95
	1-57248-037-8	How to Make a MN Will	$9.95
	1-57248-038-6	How to Start a Business in MN	$16.95
	North Carolina Backlist		
	0-913825-94-8	How to File for Divorce in NC	$19.95
	0-913825-92-1	How to Make a NC Will	$9.95
	0-913825-93-X	How to Start a Business in NC	$16.95
	Texas Backlist		
	0-913825-91-3	How to File for Divorce in TX	$19.95
	1-57248-009-2	How to Form a Simple Corporation in TX	$19.95
	0-913825-89-1	How to Make a TX Will	$9.95
	1-57248-010-6	How to Probate an Estate in TX	$19.95
	0-913825-90-5	How to Start a Business in TX	$16.95
	1-57248-012-2	How to Win in Small Claims Court in TX	$14.95
	1-57248-011-4	Landlord's Rights and Duties in TX	$19.95
		SUBTOTAL	
	IL Residents add 6.75%, FL Residents add county sales tax		
	Shipping— $4.00 for 1st book, $1.00 each additional		
		Total	

To order, call Sourcebooks at 1-800-43-BRIGHT or FAX (630)961-2168 (Bookstores, libraries, wholesalers—please call for discount)